The Family
Story Bible

Presented to

Una, Finnegan & Muirenn

From

your friends at Pilgrim United

On

March 10, 2013

The Family Story Bible

Ralph Milton

Illustrations by Margaret Kyle

Northstone

Editors: Jim Taylor and
             Mike Schwartzentruber
Cover design: Lois Huey-Heck
Illustrations: Margaret Kyle
Art Director: Robert MacDonald

Previous edition published by
Wood Lake Books Inc.

Printed in China

Northstone Publishing Inc. is an
employee-owned company, committed to
caring for the environment and all
creation. Northstone Publishing recycles,
reuses and composts, and encourages
readers to do the same. Resources are
printed on recycled paper and more
environmentally friendly groundwood
papers (newsprint), whenever possible.
The trees used are replaced through
donations to the Scoutrees for Canada
Program sponsored by Scouts Canada.
Ten percent of all profit is donated to
charitable organizations.

**Canadian Cataloguing
in Publication Data**

Milton, Ralph.
The Family Story Bible

First ed. has title: Living God's Way:
Bible stories retold for children in today's world.
ISBN 1-55145-092-5

1. Bible stories, English. I. Kyle,
Margaret. II. Title. III. Title. Living God's way.
BS551.2.M55 1996   j220.9'505   C96-910317-4

Seventh printing

Northstone Publishing Inc.
9025 Jim Bailey Road
Kelowna BC
Canada V4V 1R2

Contents

Introduction

Hebrew Scriptures

(for scripture reference see individual story)

Christian Scriptures

(for scripture reference see individual story)

Have Fun!

A Word to Adults

Reading the Bible is like participating in amateur sport. If you're not having fun, you're not doing it right.

If reading the Bible or this book is a chore, something is very wrong.

Let me explain.

I could give you a dozen important reasons why the Bible in general, and this interpretation of it in particular, would make your life easier, your experiences richer, and your teeth whiter. Believe me, I could bore you for 500 pages on that subject.

But the thing you want to know is how the Bible gets to be fun. Right?

Well, like sports, reading the Bible needs imagination and passion – and sometimes a bit of practice. And it's worth it. Without imagination and passion, sports and the Bible are both pretty boring.

I bring imagination and passion to every story in the Bible. That's my joy when I read the Bible for myself. That's my job when I approach it as a writer.

First, imagination.

Where the terse biblical text offers little detail, I add my own. Where names are missing, I invent them. Where connecting narrative is absent, I supply it. Then I add my own dash of drama and suspense and fun. Sometimes, almost the whole story comes from my imagination and almost none of it from the Bible.

If that bothers you, maybe you need to find another book.

As a professional writer, my imagination is disciplined, but it is not tamed. I do my research. The details I imagine are checked to make sure they have some textual and historical validity. I've taken a fair number of courses, done graduate work in Israel, and read hundreds of books in order to be able to do this. But still, the imagination that weaves these stories out of the raw material of the Bible is wild and childlike and some people will find that profoundly disturbing. I won't argue with them.

Second, passion.

I believe with great adult passion that God wants us to be a joyful, just, and caring people. One of the ways (but by no means the *only* way) God has chosen to do that is to encourage a particular people (the Hebrews) at a particular time (the biblical era) to record the stories of their struggles and sorrows, their joys and hopes. They collected all kinds of writings – legends, folklore, stories, poems, fiction, history, recipes and laws – into a book which we call the Bible. It is a fascinating and delightful book that has often been turned into a dry-as-dust tome by nit-picking academics, insecure preachers, and ignorant media reporters.

But the Bible can be a source of insight and wisdom and fun for adults and children. If we're open, God can speak to us through the stories of the Bible. When God speaks, it's never boring.

I'm not talking about the kind of "speaking" you hear from a few right-wing groups that claim the Bible predicts the end of the world a week from Tuesday. Nor is the Bible the voice of God telling us that everything we enjoy is indecent, immoral or fattening.

I believe, with a fire-in-the-belly passion, that the Bible contains God's call to humanity to live into the future with courage and caring, with joy and justice, with freedom and opportunity for all of creation. We're called to a radical kind of love. One of the ways we hear that call is by reading the Bible with imagination and passion.

I believe our childlike imagination

and adult passion are the keys to getting inside the real truth of the Bible stories. If that statement rings true, then I'd recommend an additional book of Bible stories – this one for adults only. It's called *Is This Your Idea of a Good Time, God?* It's written by yours truly and is published by Northstone Publishing.

One of the best ways for an adult to understand the Bible at something other than an intellectual level, is to read it with children. Some of the adult passion may be missing, but children bring a passion of their own which we can learn from. It is simple and unsophisticated, but it is real.

Imagination and passion are forms of wisdom which the biblical writers held very dear. One of the reasons I undertook this book was to learn from children who helped me see those flashes of wisdom in the Bible. Seeing these stories through the eyes of children was a wonderful education and a source of new insight. Children don't have their God-given imaginations gummed up with too much information.

When you read these stories with children, allow yourself (and encourage your child) to question, to imagine, to wonder. Give your inner child the freedom to ask, "What do you suppose happened before this...?" or, "I wonder what that person looked like...?" or, "How do you suppose that person felt...?" and especially, "I wonder what happened next...?" The answers to those questions are often not there in the Bible. We get to imagine them! Wonderful flashes of insight happen as we do that.

And the whole things turns out to be good fun.

Always remember that the stories in this book come from the Bible, but via my imagination. At times you may wonder, where is this guy coming from? So check the original story in the Bible. (If all you have is the old family Bible gathering dust on the shelf, go to a bookstore and get a new translation in today's English. I recommend either the *New Revised Standard Version* or the *Good News Bible.*) Write your own imaginative story. Enjoy doing a bit of detective work. Then make up your own mind about what the story is really about.

Try not to be "religious." The Bible is not some kind of charm that will zap you if you drop it. Don't talk about it in a kind of "stained-glass voice." The characters in the Bible were not fundamentally different than you or I. They all have warts. All of them are profoundly human.

If the Bible says something you disagree with, argue with it. If you don't believe something could have happened that way, say so. Encourage children to ask those kinds of questions too. We don't need to shift our brains into "park" when we open the Bible. We certainly don't need to handle it with kid gloves.

The Bible is not a book of rules or a set of moral precepts that we somehow absorb and then order our lives by (although some contemporary sects encourage this view). Traditional Christianity says that when we're open to the "word of God," God will speak to us *through* the Bible. So I'm suggesting that you approach the Bible with a kind of childlike openness.

I didn't come up with the idea. Jesus said it first.

So enjoy each story, whether you think it is historically true, pure fiction, or somewhere in-between. Don't turn it into a "lesson." The inner truth, the wisdom, is there *inside* the story. Don't look for some pious little moral, but be open to a flash of insight into what it means to be spiritual human beings who live in families and communities with other spiritual human beings.

Let God speak to the child in you. Enjoy!

Ralph Milton

How the Bible Came to Be

Everybody loves stories. We all like to listen to good stories. We like to tell stories about the things that happen to us.

The Bible has many kinds of things in it, but mostly it has stories. And the first part of the Bible has some of the best stories. It also has songs and rules and lots of other things.

The Hebrew people told the Bible stories many, many years ago. Often, it was the old women and old men who told the stories.

The children would listen very carefully. They heard the stories over and over. By the time the children grew up, they knew the stories by heart. Then they could tell the stories to their own children.

Each time they heard the story, the Hebrew children learned a little more about God.

The children also learned how to remember stories. That was hard sometimes. But it was important because most of the stories were not written on paper nor were they recorded on video tape. The Hebrew people wanted to be sure that when the old people died, the younger people would remember.

Even so, sometimes people would forget parts of the story, or they would make up some new parts. In this way, the stories seemed to get better and better as the years went on. And people learned more and more about God.

After a while, the Hebrew people wrote some of the stories down on long strips of animal skin which they rolled up. These were called scrolls.

A long time after that, the stories were all put together into a book we call the Bible.

The stories in the Bible are very old. Nobody knows if all the things really happened just the way they were told. Maybe some parts of the stories changed little by little as people told the story over and over.

The important thing is that every time we hear or read the stories of the Bible, we learn something about God.

That is why we often call it the Holy Bible. When we read the Bible or hear stories from the Bible, God speaks to us in a very special way.

This book is not the Bible. Many parts of the Bible are not in this book. I have chosen some of my favorite parts of the Bible and retold them in my own words.

Sometimes the stories in the Bible are very short. It seems to me that the people who first told the stories want us to fill in some of the missing parts. They want us to imagine what happened. So that's what I did.

Sometimes, I put things into the stories that I imagined. Sometimes I put things in that I think might have happened or probably happened. That's why I tell things in my stories that are not in the Bible.

At the top of each of my stories I tell you where you can find that story in the Bible itself. Why not check to see how the story is told in the Bible?

Why not pretend you are a detective? See if you can find out what parts of my story are different from the way the stories are in the Bible.

Then you could tell the story in your own words.

Ralph Milton

This is a story people told many, many years ago. They told this story, because they were trying to understand why God made the world.

God Makes a World

Genesis 1

Long, long, long ago, before there was anything, before there was a world, before there was light, before there was darkness, there was God.

Just God. All alone.

So God decided to make the world.

Then God said, "Let there be light."

So there was.

Beautiful light shining everywhere.

And God said, "That's good."

Then God said, "Let there be a sky above, and water below."

So there was.

Then God said, "Let the water come together in the hollow places, so there can be dry ground."

So there was.

And God said, "That's good."

Then God said, "Let there be green plants and tall trees and grass and beautiful flowers. And let them all make seeds so there can be new plants when the old ones die."

So there were.

And God said, "That's good."

Then God said, "Let there be a golden sun in the sky in the daytime, and a silver moon at night."

So there was.

And God said, "That's good."

Then God said, "Let there be all kinds of shiny fish in the sea and bright colored birds to fly in the air. And let the fish

have baby fish, and the birds have baby birds, so there can always be new birds and fish when the old ones die."

So there were.

And God said, "That's good."

Then God said, "Let there be animals on the land. All kinds of animals that run and crawl and gallop."

So there were.

And God said, "That's good."

Then God said, "Let there be people in the world, and let the people be made so they are like me."

So God created people. Women and men. And God said to the people, "Let there be new babies born so there will always be new people in my world when the old people die."

Then God said to the people, "Take care of my world. It's yours to use. All of it. But please be kind to my world."

Then God looked at all the world, and all the beautiful things in it.

And God said, "That's *very* good."

When it was all done, God rested.

This is a story people told many years ago. The story helped them understand why people wear clothes, why some things hurt, and why people have to work.

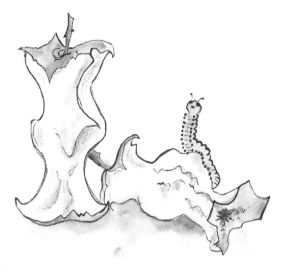

God's Beautiful Garden

Genesis 2:4 – 3:24

When God first made the world, there was nothing growing on it. It was all bare. Just soil and rocks and water.

Then God made people. God took some earth. God made it into the shape of a person. Then God breathed gently into it. And the lump of earth became a living person.

God first made two people, a man called Adam and a woman called Eve.

God gave Adam and Eve a very beautiful garden to live in. It was called the Garden of Eden. Eve and Adam walked around naked. God had given them both beautiful bodies, and they didn't mind not having any clothes to wear.

God told Eve and Adam they could eat any of the delicious fruit on the trees, or anything else that grew in the garden.

Except for one tree. God told them not to eat from one special tree, a tree that was right in the middle of the garden.

Now there was a snake in this beautiful garden. The snake liked to make trouble. So one day the snake said to Eve, "Go ahead. Eat the fruit from that special tree. It won't hurt you. Go ahead."

So Eve did. She took some of the fruit, even though she knew she shouldn't. Eve gave some of the fruit to Adam. He ate it too, even though he knew he shouldn't.

   As soon as Adam and Eve had eaten the fruit of that special
tree, they felt very badly. They felt guilty. So they tried to hide.
   Then God came to the garden, and called out,
"Where are you?"
   Adam was afraid. "I'm hiding here in the bushes because
I don't have any clothes on."
   God felt sad. God knew that Adam and Eve had eaten the
fruit of that special tree. That fruit made them think there
was something wrong with the beautiful bodies God had
given them.
   So God said to Adam and Eve. "You must leave my
beautiful garden. Because you didn't do what I asked you to
do, things will be harder for you. Your work will sometimes be
hard. You will have to grow your own food to eat. And some of
the things you have to do will hurt. You will feel pain sometimes
and you will cry."
   Then God made them some clothes out of animal skins,
and told Adam and Eve to leave the beautiful Garden of Eden.

Many, many years ago, when the Hebrew people wanted to pray to God, they would make a sacrifice. To make a sacrifice, they used something special, like really good food.

They put this food on an altar, which was a big pile of rocks. Then they put some dry wood on the rocks and lit the wood so they had a hot fire. That's where they put the food for the sacrifice. The smoke going up into the sky made them feel that God could smell the good food. "If God smells this good food," they thought, "then God won't be angry at us for our sins."

Sin is when people act and think as if they don't care about God or about themselves, or other people or about God's world.

People told this story because it helped them understand why people do wrong things. They sin. One of the worst sins is when people kill each other.

Two Brothers
Have a Fight

Genesis 4:1-16

After God told Eve and Adam to leave the Garden of Eden,
they had to work hard so they would have food to eat. Adam
and Eve planted seeds to grow food. They took care of sheep
and other animals so they would have meat to eat. It was hard,
but they were able to get enough food to stay alive.

They even had a family. Two boys. Their names were Cain
and Abel.

When Cain grew up, he worked in the fields to grow grain
and vegetables. His brother Abel looked after the sheep.

One day, the two brothers decided to make a sacrifice. Abel
worked very hard to make his sacrifice just right. He took one
of his sheep and cooked it on the altar. Abel really wanted God
to smell the good meat he was cooking.

Cain didn't really want to make a sacrifice. So Cain took
some of his grain and threw it on the fire. "That should be
good enough," he said.

God was very happy with the sacrifice that Abel had made.
But God was not happy with Cain. Cain was just pretending.
He didn't really try to make God happy.

So God told Cain, "I don't like your sacrifice. It was
just pretend."

Cain looked very sad. He felt angry at God.

God said to Cain, "Why are you looking so angry? If you
really mean it next time, I will like your sacrifice. If you don't,
that will be a sin."

Cain kept right on being angry. He asked Abel to go for a

walk with him out to the field. When nobody was looking, Cain killed Abel.

When Cain saw what he had done, he was afraid.

"Where is your brother Abel?" God asked.

"How do I know?" said Cain. "Am I supposed to look after my brother?"

"What have you done, Cain?" God said. "I can see the blood on the ground where your brother died. How could you do such a thing? Because of what you did, you will have no home to go to. Nobody will be your friend.

"When you try to grow grain and vegetables, think about your brother's blood on the ground. Because of that, it will be hard to grow things in the ground."

"I don't know what to do now," said Cain. "Nobody is my friend and nobody likes me. They will try to kill me because of what I have done to my brother."

"No, they won't," said God. "I will put a mark on you. Anyone who sees that mark will leave you alone. I don't want you being killed too."

So Cain left the place where his mother and father lived and went to live in another place, all by himself.

Here is a story about a man named Noah and his family.

People many years ago told this story because it helped them understand something called a "covenant."

When people get married, they promise to love each other. They promise to be good to each other. That is a covenant.

Some parents bring a new baby to church. The baby is baptized or dedicated. They say, "God loves us, and we love God." They promise to tell the baby about God's love. The people in the church promise to help them. That is a covenant.

When people come to join the church, they remember God's love. They promise to try their best to live in God's way. That is a covenant.

The long-ago people in the Bible knew that God had promised to be with them always. So they promised to remember God's love. That is a covenant. God's covenant.

The Bible tells us many stories about how people didn't always remember how that covenant got started. They acted as if they didn't care about God.

When that happened, someone would tell the story of Noah. Then they would remember God's covenant with them.

God Makes a Promise

Genesis 6:1 – 9:17

Noah was a very old person. Noah and his wife liked to talk with God. They and their children tried very hard to live in God's way.

It wasn't easy. All the other people in the place where the Noah family lived didn't even think about God. They fought and killed each other. They stole things and told lies. They were mean to each other. It made God very unhappy.

God became so unhappy, God finally decided to start the world all over again with new people.

So God said to Noah and his family, "Build a boat. A special kind of boat called an 'ark.'"

Then God told them how to build this ark. "It must be very big. So big that it can hold two of every kind of animal and bird in the world."

The people who didn't listen to God thought Noah was very silly. "There isn't any water anywhere near," they said. "Just dry land. That's stupid, building a boat where there isn't any water!"

Noah and his family knew it looked pretty strange. But God had told them to build this boat, so they were going to build it.

It took a long time to finish the ark. Mr. and Mrs. Noah and all their children worked at it together. When it was finally done, God told the Noah family to find two of every kind of animal and bird.

Two dogs. Two cats. Two horses. Two tigers. Two snakes. Two wallabies. Two bugs. Even two skunks. Two of everything.

It was very noisy and smelly when they had all those animals crowded into that big boat.

"Get in," God said. The Noah family got into that boat with all those animals and birds.

But the ark didn't go anywhere. It just sat there on the dry land.

"Wait," God told them gently. "Just wait."

The people who lived nearby came and laughed at how silly it all looked. Here was this huge boat, full of all those animals, with Noah and his family shut up tight inside. But there was no water. Everything was dry all around.

"Do we have to sit in this awful ark forever?" asked one of Noah's children.

"Try to be patient," said Noah. But even Noah was finding it hard to be patient.

Then, all of a sudden, it started to rain. It was almost as if God had just opened up the sky, it rained so hard. It kept raining and raining. The people left outside the ark, and all the animals that couldn't come into the ark, all died.

The ark floated up on the water and drifted around. It drifted and drifted and drifted. The Noah family

and all the animals and birds in the ark got so tired of just staying in that boat.

"Is this ark just going to float around forever?" asked one of the children.

Inside the ark it was pretty smelly. The animals would sometimes fight with each other. "This place stinks!" said the grandchildren.

Then one day, the sun came out and the wind began to blow. Noah decided to see if there was dry land anywhere. He wanted to get off that smelly ark as much as anyone.

So Noah took one of the birds, a raven, and let it fly away. But the raven came back very tired. It couldn't find any place to land. There was still water everywhere.

Then Noah tried a dove, and the same thing happened.

So the Noah family waited some more. They waited a whole week. They were getting so tired of waiting.

Then Noah tried the dove again. It flew off, and seemed to stay away a long time. When it came back, it had some olive leaves in its beak.

"Look," yelled Noah. "The dove found some leaves. That means there's some land somewhere."

Everyone cheered and all the children danced around as happy as anything. The Noah family had been on the ark for forty days and forty nights. It felt like such a long time. Now they knew it wouldn't be long before they'd be able to get off the ark and start a new life.

"The first thing we do, when we get off the ark," said Noah, "is to say 'thank you' to God."

As soon as the ark came to some dry ground, everybody got out as quickly as they could.

The Noah family piled up some rocks to make an altar. Then they put some wood on the altar and set it on fire. They put some good food on the fire and hoped the smell of the good food would go up to God. They were sure God would know they were saying "thank you!"

They let all the animals out of the boat. The animals ran around and jumped and smelled the grass and the trees. It looked as if they were saying "thank you" to God in their own way. Everyone was very happy.

God was happy too.

When people see a beautiful rainbow in the sky, they often think about God.

When people long ago saw a rainbow, they thought about God too. And they remembered the story of the Noah family. They were sure the Noah family must have seen a wonderful rainbow after it had rained so hard. Maybe the rainbow was God's way of reminding them of the covenant.

Here's a story they told about the rainbow.

God Sends a Rainbow

Genesis 9

Everyone was so glad when the rain stopped and the flood was over. Noah's grandchildren climbed out of the smelly ark and rolled around on the new grass. It was such fun.

"Well," sighed old Noah. "That was quite an adventure. I'm glad it's over."

It wasn't over. The best part of the adventure was still to come.

"I am going to make a covenant with you," said God. "This covenant will be with you and your children, and your children's children, and your children's children's children. Forever.

"My covenant is not just with you. It's with all those animals and birds you had in the ark. In fact, it's with every living thing. My covenant is with the whole world."

The Noah family must have been looking puzzled. They didn't really know what a "covenant" was. So God told them.

"This covenant means that I promise not to send any more floods to cover the whole world. Even though people forget my love, I won't destroy everything the way I did this time.

"That's *my* part of the covenant. Here's *your* part. I am giving everything to you, the people of the world. The birds that fly in the air, the animals that walk on the ground, the fish in the sea, the grass and the flowers and the trees. Everything. It's yours. Please take good care of it.

"Be good to each other. Take care of each other. I don't want any more killing. And I have a special surprise to help you remember my covenant. Look!"

Then the whole world seemed to smile a funny, upside-down kind of smile. It seemed as if everything was painted in color. The Noah family, and all the animals and birds just stopped and looked and said, "Ohhhhhh!"

"Wow!" said one of the Noah children.

It was a rainbow. A glorious rainbow in all the colors of the world. "This rainbow is the sign of my covenant," said God. "Years and years from now, when people see my rainbow, they will remember my covenant with all the people of the world and with every living thing.

"As long as there is a world,
Summer and winter,
Seed time and harvest,
When it's cold and when it's hot,
Day and night,
Whenever the sun shines through the rain,
They will remember my promise.
I will be their God.
Always! Forever!"

People long ago used to wonder, "Why do people speak different languages?"
    How come some people speak French, others English or Spanish? Some speak Urdu and others speak Cantonese. There are so many different languages. Wouldn't it be easier if everyone spoke the same language? The people of the Bible had a story about this.

The People Build a Tower

Genesis 11:1-9

After the flood in the time of Noah, people and animals and birds began to have babies. That's what God had told them to do. And these people and animals spread out all over the world.

   Some of the people found a very nice place to live. It had lots of grass for their sheep and goats. Soon more and more people came to this place and it became a city. They called the city Babylon.

   One day some of the people said, "You know what we should do? We should build a really high tower. Everybody in the whole world will come to see it. It will make us famous. We will call it the tower of Babel."

   So they started making lots of bricks, and they stuck the bricks together with tar, and they piled the bricks higher and higher.

"Our tower is going to reach right up to heaven," they said. "We are the best people in the whole world!"

God saw what the people were building. God didn't like it. "Soon they'll be able to do anything they want," said God.

So God changed the words that came out of their mouths. God changed their language, so they couldn't understand each other.

One person said "Yes," but it sounded like "no" to someone else. Or a word that sounded like "love" to one person sounded like "hate" to another. Soon they were arguing and fighting.

The people of Babylon didn't work together any more. They didn't understand each other. They stopped building the tower. They moved away from each other to many different places.

That is why, when people make sounds like talking, but we can't understand what they say, we call it "babble." We remember the story of the tower of Babel.

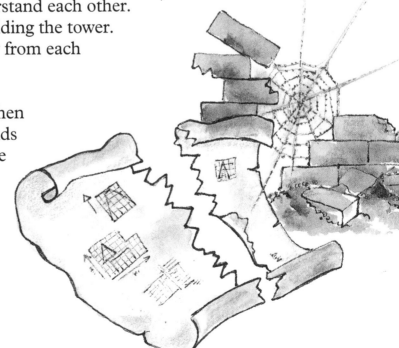

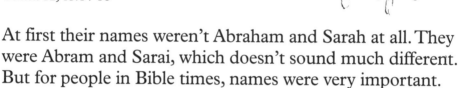

People in many parts of the world think of Abraham and Sarah as their ancestors. Ancestors are like grandparents. Except you'd have to call them great, great, great — you'd have to say "great" a thousand times — grandparents. Jewish people, Moslem people and Christian people all think of Abraham and Sarah in this way.

The stories about Abraham and Sarah are very, very old. All the things they did take many stories to tell.

Abraham and Sarah Begin a Journey

Genesis 12, 13:14-18

At first their names weren't Abraham and Sarah at all. They were Abram and Sarai, which doesn't sound much different. But for people in Bible times, names were very important.

Abram and Sarai lived in a city called Haran. They liked living there. One day they had a big surprise.

God told Abram and Sarai to move. Just like that.

"Go away from your mother and father. Go away from all the nice things you have in Haran. Just go. I'll tell you where, later."

That was a hard thing to do. But Abram and Sarai loved God very much, so they went.

Their nephew Lot went with them. Sarai and Abram were quite rich. They took all their cows and their sheep and their tents. They took many people to help them care for all their animals and things.

It was like a camping trip with lots of people. Except it probably wasn't very much fun. Abram and Sarai and the rest would walk a long way. Then they would set up all their tents. After a while, they would go somewhere else. Sometimes it was hot. Or dusty. Sometimes they hurt their feet on the sharp stones.

They went to a place called Shechem, where Abram built an altar to offer sacrifices to God.

Then they went to Bethel, then to Ai, then to Negev and even all the way to Egypt. They just kept traveling and traveling.

When Abram and Sarai would talk to each other at night, just before they went to sleep, they would wonder, "Why doesn't God tell us where we are going?"

Each time they remembered that when God had said, "Go," God had also made them a promise.

"Your children's children's children's children will be a great nation. People will remember you for years and years. They will remember you and what you have done. People all over the world will learn to live in God's way because of you."

Abram and Sarai tried very hard to believe God's promise. It was so hard though, because they didn't have any children.

"How can God's promise come true when we don't have a baby?" wondered Abram.

"Sometimes it's so hard to believe and trust God," said Sarai.

Abram and Sarai's family was very large. Today we think of a family as having two or three, perhaps six or seven people.

Sarai and Abram's family was different. There were uncles and aunts and cousins and many servants. There may have been more than a hundred people. Their nephew Lot also had a family that was just as big.

Abram and Lot Solve a Problem

Genesis 13

Abram and Sarai sometimes felt as if they had camped in just about every place in the world. They knew God had told them they would be shown where they should live. So far, God hadn't shown them.

Abram and Sarai wondered what God wanted them to do. In the meantime, their family got bigger. The aunts and uncles and cousins had babies. The sheep and goats had baby sheep and goats. Abram and Sarai got more people to help them take care of all the animals.

The same thing happened with Lot's family.

It was hard to find enough grass for all the animals to eat and enough water for them to drink. Sometimes, the people who helped Lot got into arguments with the people who helped Abram and Sarai.

"Stay away from our grass," they shouted. "We got here first."

"So what? Our animals need to eat too."

"But there isn't enough grass for all of them."

Soon Abram began to think, "We'd better do something, or they'll start fighting."

So Abram and Lot had a talk.

"Lot," said Abram "there are too many of us. Too many

people and too many animals. Why don't we split up?"

"Whatever you say, Uncle Abram," said Lot.

"You go wherever you like," said Abram. "Take all your animals and all the people who help you look after them. I'll go the other way."

Lot looked around. "I think I'll go to the Jordan valley," said Lot. "It has nice green grass and plenty of water for all my animals."

"That's fine," said Abram. Then Abram and Sarai looked the other way. There wasn't much grass and hardly any water up in the hills. There was lots of rock and sand.

As they were walking, God told Abram and Sarai where to stay.

"Here it is," said God. "This is home. This is where you are going to live. And remember what I promised. You will have so many great, great, great, grandchildren, as many as there are little grains of sand. That many!"

Abram and Sarai could see lots of grains of sand. It didn't look like a very nice place to live. Still, they were glad to stop moving around. But they had a hard time believing God's promise about all those grandchildren.

"I'm too old to have any children now," Sarai groaned. "How can I have babies when I'm old enough to be a grandmother?"

"I'm old enough to be a grandfather." Abram shook his head. "It's very hard to believe God's promise."

"Well, I believe God's promise." Sarai took a big, deep breath. "So, let's start unpacking."

Hagar Hears God's Promise

based on Genesis 16:1-16 & 21:8-21

Hagar wanted something of her very own.

She'd never had anything that belonged to her. Not even her clothes. Not even her own self.

Hagar was a slave. A slave is someone who is owned by somebody else, the way you might own a dog or a cat. Hagar's owner was Sarah. Sarah was married to Abraham.

Sarah wanted a baby. God had promised her a baby, but she was getting old and she started to worry that maybe there would never be a baby. So Sarah had a plan. In those days, if a woman could not have a baby, she could ask another woman to help her.

"Abraham," Sarah said one day, "I want you to have sex with my slave, Hagar, so that she will have our baby. Because Hagar is my slave, the baby will belong to me and it will be as if the baby really came out of my body."

So that's what happened. Sarah and Abraham didn't ask Hagar if it was okay. They just went and did it.

When Hagar got pregnant she felt important. People said nice things and talked about her baby. But sometimes she teased Sarah. "I can have a baby and you can't." Then Sarah got so angry that Hagar had to run away.

But God talked with Hagar when she was hiding from Sarah. "Hagar, right now you have to think of your baby. Go back and live with Sarah and do what she tells you. But remember this Hagar. You will give birth to a child of the promise. A good name for the child would be Ishmael, which means, 'God hears.' God hears you, Hagar, and God will hear Ishmael, and from you will come a great nation of many people."

Then Hagar said to God, "I don't know your name, but I will call you, 'The God of Seeing.' That will be your name from me and for Ishmael and for all the people of the promise." So Hagar went back to live with Sarah, even though it was a hard thing to do.

When the baby came out of Hagar's body, she knew it was *her* baby, but Sarah told her friends, "See! *I* have a baby now." Then Hagar felt as if everything had been taken away from her again.

One day, Sarah had a baby of her own. She named him Isaac. God talked to Sarah and Abraham about their baby too, and told them Isaac would also be the father of a great nation of people. That made them very, very happy.

It made Hagar very worried, because she knew that meant danger for Ishmael. Hagar began to wonder if God really had made that promise, or whether she had just been dreaming.

One day Ishmael and Isaac were playing together. Sarah saw them and called Abraham, "Get that kid and his mother out of here. I don't want him playing with my Isaac. God has promised to make Isaac's descendants into a great nation, so we don't need Ishmael any more. The promise is just for us!"

"But Sarah," said Abraham. "You wanted Ishmael for your own son before Isaac came. I can't just kick them out. Where would they go?"

"Just get rid of them!" shouted Sarah.

So Abraham gave Hagar a leather bag of water and some food and told her to go with Ishmael into the desert. Hagar could hardly believe that Abraham and Sarah would do such a thing. There was no food or people or anything out in the desert.

Soon the food and water were gone. Hagar tried so hard to keep going, but Ishmael got weaker and weaker. He couldn't walk anymore.

Hagar put Ishmael under a bush and walked away. She couldn't bear to hear him cry. She didn't want to watch him die.

Hagar felt angry at God. "Why did you let this happen to us?" she yelled. "Why God? Why do we have to die like this?"

"Hagar!" God spoke gently inside her. "Sarah and Abraham don't understand. The promise is not just for *one* person or *one* tribe. The promise is for you and Ishmael too. Ishmael will get married and you will have grandchildren and many, many great-grandchildren."

Hagar began to cry. Until now, she had been too angry to cry, but when she heard God's voice in her heart, she began to believe the promise again. She remembered how she had talked with God when she ran away from Sarah, how she had given God a name, and God had given her a name for Ishmael, and how God had made a promise to her.

And then, through her tears, Hagar saw a well. Water! There in the desert!

Hagar ran and got Ishmael. She put some water on his dry lips and got him to drink. Soon he began to feel strong again. Then Hagar drank, and she felt strong too. Again, she was able to believe God's promise.

"Ishmael," she said. "All my life I wanted something of my very own. Now I have it. I have God's promise. We both have God's promise, Ishmael, and we have each other. We are not slaves anymore. We are free to be God's children."

Then Hagar stood up tall. She raised her arms up wide to the whole sky.

In a strong, quiet voice, Hagar said, "Thank you, God."

A Mother of Nations

Genesis 17 – 18:19, 21:1-7

God repeated the promise to Abram and Sarai many times. Each time it was the same promise.

Each year it got harder and harder to believe the promise, because each year Sarai and Abram got older and older.

One day God said to Abram. "Remember my promise. Always remember. And because of my promise, I want you to change your name."

"Right now your name is Abram, which means 'important father.' But from now on, your name will be 'Abraham' which means 'the father of many.'

"And Sarai should change her name too. Call her 'Sarah' which means 'Princess.' Sarah will be the mother of many nations."

Abraham told Sarah about his talk with God. "But how can that be," he said. "I'm too old to be anybody's father."

Then one day, when Sarah was working inside the tent and Abraham was sitting under a tree outside, they had some visitors. Sarah looked out through the door of the tent. "Are they sent by God?" she wondered.

Abraham and Sarah were always kind to visitors when they

came. So Sarah baked some bread and Abraham got some meat, and soon they had a nice meal ready.

After the meal, while Abraham and the three visitors sat under the tree outside the tent, one of the visitors said something hard to believe.

"I'll be coming back this way in about a year," he said. "By then, Sarah will have had a baby."

Sarah was listening inside the tent. At first she just giggled a little at the idea of it. A woman, as old as a grandmother, having a baby. Then she started to laugh. She laughed so hard she could hardly stop.

"Why is Sarah laughing?" said the man. "Is anything too hard for God?"

"Oh, I didn't laugh," said Sarah.

"You laughed all right," said the man. "But remember, a year from now, you'll have a baby."

When they heard this Sarah and Abraham both laughed until their sides ached.

Then one day it happened. Sarah became pregnant. Even though she was very old, she had a baby.

She and Abraham were so happy as they looked at their tiny baby boy, with his little fists and his tightly closed eyes.

So they gave their baby a special name. They called him Isaac, which means "laughter."

God's promise was coming true after all. Sarah and Abraham knew this as they smiled at the little baby in their arms.

They would become great, great, great, great grandparents. And all because of God's promise and a baby named Isaac. A baby named Laughter.

This story is scary. It would be best to read it with an adult and then talk about it afterwards.

In Bible times, some people thought God wanted them to hurt other people. Sometimes they thought God wanted them to kill other people in wars. God never wants that.

Sometimes adults think it's OK to hurt children or each other. That isn't true. God never wants people to hurt each other. That's one of the reasons this story is in the Bible.

Abraham Doesn't Understand

Genesis 22

Sarah and Abraham loved Isaac very much. Isaac was the only child they had, born when they were both very old.

Sometimes Abraham and Sarah would say to each other, "We are very rich people. We own lots of sheep and goats and we have many people working for us. But we'd give them all away to keep Isaac."

Sarah and Abraham loved Isaac. They loved God too. They always tried so hard to do whatever God wanted them to do.

Often they would have a sacrifice for God. They would take a lamb or a goat. Then they would build a big fire on a pile of rocks they called an altar. They would kill the lamb or goat and burn it on the fire. Abraham and Sarah felt this was a good way to show their love for God.

One day God called, "Abraham."

"I'm here, God," said Abraham.

"I want you to take your son, Isaac, whom you love so much. Go to a place called Moriah, where I will show you a mountain. There I want you to make a sacrifice, but I want you to use Isaac, not a lamb or a goat."

Abraham could hardly believe God would want him to do such a thing. He cried all night long, and asked God over and over again, "Please, not Isaac. You can have anything I own, but please, not Isaac. He's our only child."

In the morning, Abraham knew that he had to do it. So he got some wood, and a sharp knife, and a burning torch to light the fire. Abraham also asked two of his servants to help carry things. And of course, he took Isaac.

They traveled for two days and two nights. On the third day while they were walking, Abraham told the servants to stay behind. "Isaac and I will go up the mountain and make our sacrifice," he said. "Wait here, please."

"Dad," Isaac asked, "we have wood for the sacrifice, and we have a torch to light the fire. How come we don't have a lamb or a goat for the sacrifice?"

Abraham seemed to take a long time to answer Isaac's question. Then he said, "God will give us something for the sacrifice."

Isaac didn't understand, but he didn't mind. He often didn't understand the things his dad said about God.

When they finally got to the right place, Abraham took the wood and piled it on the altar.

Then Abraham took Isaac in his arms and gave him a long, long hug. Very quietly and gently he said, "Isaac, my son, I love you so very, very much. I want you to know that, Isaac."

"I know that, Father," said Isaac. "And I love you too."

Then Abraham tied Isaac with some ropes. "Why are you doing that?" Isaac asked.

Abraham didn't say anything, but he kissed Isaac very gently, and put him on top of the altar. Isaac could hear his dad say some quiet words, as if Abraham was praying.

Then all of a sudden, Abraham pulled off the ropes. He picked up Isaac and hugged him. There were tears streaming down Abraham's face, but he was smiling.

"Isaac. Oh, Isaac my son," Abraham said. "Look over there. In the bush. There's a sheep God has given us for the sacrifice."

"But Dad, why did you tie me up on the altar. Were you going to sacrifice me?"

"Yes, Isaac. It was a test. I had to be willing to give up my most precious thing to prove that I loved God. That's what God told me to do."

"But you didn't," said Isaac.

"No," said Abraham. "Just when I was going to do it, an angel said to me, 'Abraham, don't you touch that boy! Now I know that you love God more than anything.' I was so happy to hear that message from God. Now I know I can love you, Isaac, and love God too.

"I also learned something else. God doesn't want us to hurt each other."

So Abraham and Isaac took the sheep that was caught in the bush, and they made a sacrifice to God. As part of their sacrifice they said "Thank you, God."

Then once more, God told Abraham about the promise. "You will have more great, great, great, great grandchildren than there are stars in the sky. They will remember you, Abraham. They will remember that you were willing to give up anything, even your son Isaac, for God."

Rebecca and Isaac

Genesis 24

Sarah was a hundred and twenty-seven years old when she died. Isaac was a grown man by this time. He cried when his mother died. Isaac and his father, Abraham, buried her in a special place which they bought from some of the people who lived nearby.

Before Sarah died, she and Isaac and Abraham had some long talks about God's promise. Now Isaac remembered those talks with his mother and he felt very lonely.

"Isaac," said Abraham. "You need to get married."

"But Dad… " Isaac started to say.

"Never mind. Do what I say. You can't marry any of the women around here," Abraham said. "They don't live in God's way. They don't understand about God's promise."

"But Dad… " Isaac tried again.

"Just be quiet and listen," said Abraham. "I'll send one of my servants to the place where we used to live, long before you were born, Isaac. We have lots of uncles and aunts and cousins living there. They don't know about God's promise, but they try to live in God's way. Maybe the servant can find the right person for you to marry."

So Abraham sent one of his servants, a man named Eliezer, to the town of Nahor where Abraham's relatives still lived. He made Eliezer promise to find just the right woman. To help the servant, Abraham sent along ten camels loaded down with good things. These were gifts Eliezer could give to Abraham's relatives.

When Eliezer got to Nahor, he was hot and tired. He stopped to rest in the shade of some trees that grew near a well. While he was resting, Eliezer watched the people come to the well to get water.

The servant prayed to God, "Please help me choose the right person." Just then he saw Rebecca coming to the well.

"Could you give me a drink of water?" he said to Rebecca.

"Of course," she said. And then without being asked, she gave water to all ten camels too.

That was hard work, because camels drink lots and lots of water. The well was very deep. She was quite tired by the time she finished. But she didn't mind. Rebecca felt it was important to be kind to strangers. She often offered to help people when they seemed to need it.

The servant smiled as he watched Rebecca carry water to his camels. "I think this is the woman God would like me to bring to Isaac, so they can share the promise together."

"Thank you," said Abraham's servant, when Rebecca had finished. "Is there room at your house for me to spend the night?"

"Of course," said Rebecca. "We've got lots of room and food for you and for your camels."

There was lots to talk about at Rebecca's house that night. They invited Eliezer to have supper with them. Before he would eat, he had to tell them all the news about Abraham and Sarah and Isaac. And of course, he explained why he had come.

"I think God wants me to invite Rebecca to share the promise with Isaac," Eliezer said.

Rebecca's mother, and her brother, and all the rest of the family didn't know what to think. They talked about whether Rebecca should go, or she shouldn't go. Nobody said, "Let's go ask Rebecca."

Finally they all agreed. Rebecca should go. That's when Eliezer brought out all the wonderful gifts he had brought. He gave them all to Rebecca's family.

They all talked as if it didn't matter what Rebecca thought. The next day someone said, "Maybe we should ask Rebecca."

So they did.

"I'll go," said Rebecca. "Right now."

"Right now?" said her mother. "Couldn't you wait for a week or so?"

"No, I want to go right now," Rebecca insisted.

The servant smiled to himself. "She can think for herself," he thought. "She's not only got a strong body, she's got a strong spirit too. Rebecca and Isaac will like each other."

The next morning they all left. The servant and his helpers and all ten camels, and Rebecca and all her helpers. There were lots of hugs and tears and goodbyes, and then they set off.

It took many days to get to where Isaac lived in Canaan. Rebecca didn't like riding on camels one bit. Sometimes she felt sick because the camels would sway back and forth. Once she had to throw up. Sometimes she hated the smell of the camels. Sometimes she was just plain bored. It was a long trip.

One day Eliezer told her, "We're getting close to Canaan now." Rebecca began to get excited. When she saw a man walking in a field she asked Eliezer, "Who's that?"

"That," said Eliezer, "is Isaac. He's the man you have come to marry."

"Make the camel kneel so I can get off," said Rebecca. Then she began walking across the field toward Isaac.

Isaac saw Rebecca coming across the field. They had never seen each other before, and yet they knew they were going to be husband and wife.

Both Rebecca and Isaac had thought of things they would say to each other when they met. Now neither could think of anything. They walked together toward the tent where Sarah, Isaac's mother, had lived.

Rebecca and Isaac were married in that tent.

In time they came to love each other very deeply. And Rebecca often thanked God because of the promise that she and Isaac shared.

Rebecca and Her Babies

Genesis 25

After Rebecca and Isaac were married, they began hoping for a baby. It didn't happen.

Sometimes Rebecca would say to Isaac, "I'm beginning to know what your mom felt like. She was ninety years old before you came along. Will I have to wait that long?"

Rebecca didn't wait quite that long. Twenty years after they were married, she said to her husband, "Isaac, we're pregnant."

She didn't have an easy time. Rebecca knew she would feel the baby moving inside her, but it seemed this baby was jumping around far too much.

So Rebecca asked God about it. God gave her a bigger answer than she expected.

"You are having twins, Rebecca," said God. "Each of the twins will grow up to be the grandparent of many people, the great-great-grandparent of a whole nation. It's part of the promise I made to Abraham and Sarah."

When the twins were born, they turned out to be two boys. The first one to be born seemed all red and hairy. They named him Esau, which means "hairy."

The second twin came out of Rebecca right after the first. He came so close, he seemed to be hanging onto the heel of his brother. So they named him Jacob, which means "he grabs what doesn't belong to him."

As the boys grew older, Esau liked to go out hunting for food in the hills. That made Isaac, his father, happy. Jacob liked to stay around home with his mother, so Rebecca liked him the best.

Esau and Jacob often got angry at each other. "I'm the oldest," said Esau. "Father will give me everything when he dies. You won't get anything."

It was true. Esau was older by about one minute. In those days, the oldest son got almost everything when his father died. Younger sons got just a little. Girls didn't get anything.

"It's not fair," Rebecca often said to Jacob. "You should have your father's sheep and cows and goats. We've got to figure out a way to make it happen."

One day Jacob was cooking up a tasty stew for himself and Rebecca. It smelled wonderful. Jacob was a good cook.

Just then Esau came in from hunting. He hadn't caught anything, so he hadn't eaten for two days. He was very, very hungry. "Give me some of your stew!" he said to Jacob.

Now Jacob saw his chance. "I'll give you some of my stew if you promise to let me have all the things Dad plans to give to you."

"Who cares?" Esau yelled. "You can have anything you want. If I don't eat right away, I'll die anyway."

"Promise?" asked Jacob.

"Yes, promise! Now give me some food."

Jacob smiled. He knew he would get something that didn't belong to him. He ran to tell his mother about it.

Esau didn't think about what he had just done. He was too busy eating.

Jacob Steals from Esau

Genesis 27

"I don't think Esau even remembers what he promised you," Rebecca said one day.

"But a promise is a promise," said Jacob.

"Maybe," said Rebecca, "but your father, Isaac, doesn't know about it. And one day he will give Esau his blessing. That means everything he has, all his goats and his sheep and everything, will belong to Esau. Esau will get everything, even though Esau said you would have it."

"So what can we do?"

"I'm not sure," said Rebecca. "But I'm always near your father. He's so old and blind now. I have to take care of him all the time. I'll look for a chance."

One day it happened. "Tell Esau I want to talk to him," old Isaac said to Rebecca. So Rebecca went and called Esau. Then she stood outside of their tent and listened to what Isaac said.

"Esau, my son." Isaac took Esau's hairy hands into his. "I am getting very old. I can't see any more, and I can't walk. I think I am going to die soon. Before I die, I want to give you my blessing."

"Oh now, Father," said Esau. "You're not going to die. You'll be able to see again."

"It's all right," said Isaac. "I have had a good life and I am ready to die. Now go out and hunt something to eat. Bring it back here and make a tasty dinner for me. When I've eaten the food, I'll give you my blessing."

"Yes, Father." Esau ran off to get his bow and arrows. Rebecca ran off to find Jacob.

"Listen, Jacob." Rebecca talked very fast. "Go get a goat quickly. Kill it so I can cook it just the way your dad likes it. And here. Tie this goat skin on your neck and on your hands so you feel as hairy as Esau. Get some of Esau's clothes so you smell like him too."

Jacob took the food in and tried to trick his dad. "I'm back, Dad," he said, trying to make his voice sound like Esau's, "God helped me catch something very fast, so I cooked it just the way you like it."

Old Isaac reached out to touch Jacob as he gave him the food. "Your voice sounds like Jacob," Isaac said. "But your hands feel like Esau's."

Then the old man ate the food. He still wasn't quite sure it was Esau, so he said, "Come close to me so I can kiss you." When Jacob came close, Isaac could smell Esau's clothes, the clothes of a hunter. Then he thought it really was Esau.

So Isaac blessed Jacob, thinking it was Esau.

"May God give you every good thing," he said. "May the promise that God made to your grandparents, Sarah and Abraham, be your promise too. And everything that I own is yours, my son."

Soon after Jacob got up and left, Esau came in. "Here is the food I have cooked for you," he said.

"Who are you?" Isaac asked.

"I am Esau, your oldest son. I have come for your blessing."

Isaac started to shake all over. "Who was it that just brought me some food? Because whoever it was, I have given him my blessing."

"It's that Jacob again," yelled Esau. "He keeps taking what doesn't belong to him! He cheats me out of everything!"

"Yes," said Isaac. "Your brother came and lied to me, and he took your blessing."

"Can't you give me a blessing too?" Esau asked. He was crying now. "Please, Dad, can't you bless me too?"

"No, Esau, I can't. I'm so sorry, but I can't. What I have done, I have done. I can't change it."

Esau was very, very angry. "I'm going to kill Jacob for what he did," he thought to himself. "I'm going to kill him."

Rebecca knew how angry Esau was. So she said to Jacob, "You have to run away. Go right now."

"But where can I go, mother?" asked Jacob.

"Go to my brother Laban who lives in Haran. Go stay with him until Esau stops being angry. Then you can come back home."

So Jacob ran away to Haran.

Jacob had cheated his brother. Now his father was very sad. His brother was angry. His mother had told him to run away. He wouldn't get his father's sheep and goats after all.

Jacob wasn't very happy. And Rebecca cried because Jacob wasn't home anymore.

Jacob's Dream

Genesis 28:10-22

Jacob was running away. He had cheated his brother and lied to his father. He was afraid.

Jacob's mother, Rebecca, had told him to run to Haran, to the place where her brother Laban lived. But Jacob didn't even know where Haran was.

Jacob ran and ran until he was so tired, he could hardly stand up. It was getting dark and he was afraid. Over and over he thought about what he had done.

Jacob knew that Isaac's blessing meant God's promise of a great nation was now his. God had made the promise to Abraham and Sarah, then it had been passed on to Rebecca and Isaac.

Now it was his. But as Jacob stood there alone in the dark, feeling cold and hungry, God's promise didn't seem to help very much.

Finally,
Jacob was so
tired, he lay down
on the hard ground.
He put his head on a rock.
"Some pillow," he thought to
himself. In the middle of the night,
something happened.
Maybe it was just a dream.

Jacob didn't think it was a dream
because it was all so real. Jacob was sure he saw
a bright light from up in the sky. Then there were
stairs that began right beside him on the ground, and
reached all the way up into the sky.

"There were angels on the stairs," Jacob told his
children many years later. "Angels going up the stairs, and
angels coming down. And at the very top, there was God.

"Then God spoke to me," said Jacob. "God said, 'I am the
God of your grandparents, Abraham and Sarah, and of your
parents, Isaac and Rebecca. The promise is now yours,
Jacob. You will be the great-great-grandfather of many, many
people. People all over the world will learn about me, because
of you. And Jacob, I will be with you. I am your God. I will
take care of you.'"

The next morning Jacob woke up. Well, he wasn't sure if he woke up because he wasn't sure if he had been sleeping. But he did remember what he had seen. Or dreamed.

So Jacob took the stone he had used for a pillow, and he set it up on end. "This place is special, because I've seen God here," Jacob said to himself.

"I'm going to call this place Bethel, which means, 'the house of God.' And from now on, I will give one-tenth of everything I own to God."

The next morning, as Jacob walked along, he thought and thought about God's promise, and about what kind of person God wanted him to be.

Jacob still didn't know where Haran was. He was still alone and hungry. All he had were the clothes on his back and his walking stick.

But somehow, Jacob felt much better after his strange experience the night before.

Jacob Falls in Love

Genesis 29

Jacob walked a long, long time, through some strange countries. Then he saw some people and a flock of sheep around a well.

"Hello!" said Jacob. "Do you know the way to Haran?"

"Yes," said the shepherds, "we live in Haran."

"Oh," said Jacob. "Then do you know a man named Laban?"

"Sure we do."

"Can you tell me the way to his house?" asked Jacob. "Laban is my uncle."

"We can do even better than that." One of the shepherds pointed to some sheep coming toward the well. "The person leading those sheep is Rachel, one of Laban's daughters."

Jacob didn't know what to say or do. But he could see that Rachel had come to the well to give her sheep a drink. Jacob ran over to the well, and moved the stone covering the well. It was a huge stone.

"Look at that man move that stone," said one of the other shepherds. "How come he's strong enough to move it all by himself?"

"He must be in love," said another shepherd.

Jacob gave a drink to all of Rachel's sheep. Then he gave her a kiss. Then he started to cry.

Rachel didn't know what to think. She ran home and told her father.

In those days, a woman and a man couldn't just decide to marry each other. They had to ask the woman's father. Fathers felt their daughters belonged to them. Fathers wouldsometimes sell their daughters the way they might sell a sheep or a goat.

Jacob didn't have anything except his clothes and his walking stick. He knew he had nothing to give Rachel's father. So Jacob went to Rachel's father and asked for a job.

Jacob began to work for Laban taking care of the sheep and goats. He worked very hard.

After Jacob had been working for Laban for a whole month, he said, "I want to marry Rachel. I love her very much. If I work for you for seven years, can I marry her?"

"Sure," said Laban.

Jacob didn't know that Laban was not very honest. In fact, Laban liked to trick people. Like Jacob, Laban tried to grab things that didn't belong to him.

So Jacob worked hard for seven years. Finally, it was time for the wedding. He was very excited when he saw the bride coming to him.

Jacob wanted to see her eyes. "I wonder if she is as happy and excited as I am?" he thought. But her face was covered with a dark veil. That's what brides always wore in those days.

The wedding party lasted far into the night. The next morning when Jacob woke up, he found himself in bed with Leah, Rachel's older sister.

Jacob was very angry. Leah was a nice person, but Jacob was in love with Rachel.

"Why have you done this to me?" Jacob yelled at Laban. "I worked seven years so I could marry Rachel. Now you made Leah marry me. Why?"

"In our country, the younger daughter can't get married until the older daughter is married," said Laban. "Rachel can't get married until Leah is married."

"So what should I do?" asked Jacob.

"It's simple," Laban laughed. "You can marry more than one woman. Go ahead. You can marry Rachel now, too. Then you can work for seven more years to pay for her."

"Well, all right," Jacob shrugged.

Then Jacob's eyes got very big. He knew what had happened. He had been tricked. Just as Jacob had tricked his brother, now Jacob had been tricked.

Neither Laban nor Jacob even wondered how Leah and Rachel felt about all this.

Esau Forgives

Genesis 31, 32 & 33

Jacob and Rachel and Leah stayed with Laban a long time.
They had lots of children. There was a girl named Dinah and
eleven boys.

All of them worked hard. They took good care of the goats
and sheep and donkeys. The family became quite rich.

One day, God told Jacob it was time to go back to his home.
Jacob was afraid when God said this. Jacob remembered the
tricks he had played on his brother Esau.

"Maybe," he thought, "if I give lots of presents to my
brother...maybe he won't be angry any more."

So Rachel and Leah and Jacob and all their children and all
the people who helped them, and all the sheep and goats and
donkeys began to move back to Canaan. There were so many,
it looked like a whole town moving all at once.

Jacob was still very worried. Sometimes he was afraid that
Esau would kill him. Sometimes Jacob was really sorry for what
he had done.

One night Jacob had asked all the others to go ahead a little
ways. "I just want to be by myself tonight," he said.

Jacob never forgot that night. Jacob wasn't sure if it was a
dream or not, but if it was a dream, it was a real nightmare.

Jacob seemed to be fighting with someone. Or something.
When he tried to go one way, it felt as if someone was holding
him. Sometimes Jacob felt as if he was fighting with himself.
Sometimes it felt as if he was fighting with the wrong things
he had done. Sometimes Jacob felt as if he was fighting
with God.

Jacob fought all night. Just before morning, he screamed in

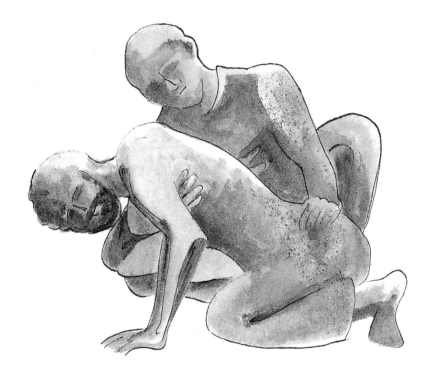

pain. Whoever, or whatever he was fighting with, touched the top of his leg and hurt him badly.

Then it seemed as if the fighting was over, and Jacob could talk with whoever it was.

"What is your name?" this strange person seemed to ask.

"My name is Jacob."

"Now your name will be changed. Your name won't be Jacob any more. Your name will be Israel, which means, 'you struggled with God and with other people.'"

Just then, the sun began to rise. Jacob wasn't sure if it had been a dream or not. Then he realized it couldn't all have been a dream, because his leg was very sore and it was hard to walk.

Very soon after that, Jacob sent many sheep and goats and donkeys ahead to Esau, hoping Esau wouldn't be angry any more.

When Jacob saw Esau coming, he saw a smile on Esau's face. Esau threw his arms around his brother, and gave him a big hug and a kiss. And then they both had a good cry. They knew they could be brothers again. Jacob knew that God had forgiven him because Esau forgave him.

Often at night, Jacob would lie awake thinking about all the things that had happened. Jacob would think about that night when he had a fight with the angel. Or was it an angel? Jacob was never sure.

But Jacob knew that part of the fighting had been with the part in himself that was running away from God. He had told many lies and cheated many people. Jacob knew that was wrong.

Jacob wondered how God's promise could still be with a person like him who didn't seem to be living in God's way. Then he thought about his new name, Israel. Somehow Jacob knew that the name was not just for him alone, but for his whole family. It was for Leah and Rachel, for all their children and for all the people who helped them.

They would be called, "the house of Israel," the people who had struggled with God... the people who had struggled to know God's promise.

Rachel Dies Having a Baby

Genesis 35

There were quite a lot of people in the house of Israel. By this time, some of the children had grown up and there were grandchildren.

They lived in tents and moved from place to place. They were always looking for nice green grass where the sheep and goats and donkeys could eat.

Rachel and Leah liked to talk to each other. Rachel sometimes asked, "How come you have such an easy time having babies, Leah? It's always so hard for me."

Of course, Leah didn't know the answer. She always tried to help her sister. Rachel had one baby while they were still living with Laban, their father. The baby's name was Joseph.

Rachel wanted to have more babies. One day she gave Leah a big hug. "Leah. Guess what? I'm pregnant!" The two sisters did a little dance, they were so happy.

But when the baby came, they were not happy. Rachel had a very hard time when this baby was being born. Leah and the other women who were helping did everything they could, but Rachel died.

Leah and Jacob were very sad when this happened. Both of them had loved Rachel very much. They buried Rachel in the ground and put a big stone to mark the place.

This happened near the town of Bethlehem. For many years people remembered Rachel when they saw the stone over her grave.

Though Rachel died, the baby was fine. It was a boy, and they named him Benjamin.

There was other sadness in the house of Israel. Old grandpa Isaac had lived for a hundred and eighty years. He was very old. Isaac didn't mind dying because he said, "I have had a good life."

Jacob and Esau cried anyway. Jacob cried because he remembered how he had hurt his father with the things he had done. Still, Jacob was glad he'd had a chance to say, "I'm sorry." He was glad he had told his father how much he loved him.

Joseph's Coat of Many Colors

Genesis 37

Jacob and Leah and their family settled down in the land of Canaan.

The "house of Israel" had many animals to look after. Their twelve sons had to take them to many different places to find grass. Well, not all of the twelve sons.

Joseph, the first baby that Rachel had, was his dad's favorite. Jacob always treated Joseph best of all. The other brothers didn't like that one bit.

Joseph wasn't always very kind to his brothers either. Jacob gave Joseph a very nice coat. It had pretty colors and long sleeves. It was much nicer than the clothes the other brothers had. Sometimes Joseph would show off his fancy coat, just to get his brothers angry.

Joseph had dreams, and he loved to tell his brothers all about them. He loved thinking of what the dreams meant. In those days, people thought dreams could tell you what was going to happen.

"Guess what I dreamed last night?" Joseph said one day. "I dreamed we were working out in the field tying bundles of grain together. All your bundles came and bowed down to my bundle."

"I suppose," snapped one of the brothers, "that means someday you are going to be our boss."

"That's right," laughed Joseph.

Joseph even made his father angry. "I had a dream in which the sun and the moon and eleven stars bowed down to me."

"Are you trying to tell us that you will be the boss over me and your mother and all your brothers?" Jacob growled.

One day, all the brothers except Joseph had taken all the animals far away from home to find grass. They had been gone for a long time. Old Jacob worried about them.

"Go and find your brothers," Jacob said to Joseph. "Find out if they're all right. Then come back and tell me."

It was a long walk for Joseph to find his brothers. When they saw him coming in his bright new coat, they felt angry.

"Here comes the dreamer," they said. "He thinks he's so smart. Let's fix him."

So the brothers grabbed Joseph and tore off his fancy coat. Then they threw him into a deep hole. Some of the brothers wanted to kill Joseph. Reuben, the oldest brother, said "No!"

Just then they saw some people coming along. They were traders, people who buy things from one person and sell the things to somebody else. The traders even sold slaves.

A slave is a person who belongs to somebody, the way you might own a dog or a cat.

So the brothers went up to the traders and said, "Would you like to buy a slave? Cheap?"

They sold Joseph to the traders, who took him to a faraway country called Egypt.

"Now what will we tell Father?" the brothers wondered.

"Let's tell Father that a wild animal killed Joseph," said one of them. So they killed one of their sheep and put the blood all over Joseph's coat. Then they tore holes in the coat.

When they got back home, they showed Joseph's torn and bloody coat to Jacob.

Old Jacob just cried and cried and cried. Nothing the brothers did could make Jacob stop crying. The brothers knew they had done a terrible thing.

Joseph Helps the Pharaoh

Genesis 40 & 41

Joseph walked for many, many days. The traders made him walk along behind their camels. If he walked a little bit too slow, one of the traders would hit him hard.

Joseph was very afraid. He didn't know where he was going or what would happen to him.

The traders took him to another country, a country called Egypt. There the traders sold Joseph to one of the rich people.

Joseph worked very hard. He tried to be a very good slave.

Joseph not only worked hard, he also knew about dreams. When he was at home, Joseph often understood his own dreams. Here in Egypt, he helped people understand what their dreams meant.

One day the king of Egypt asked Joseph to help him understand some dreams. The king of Egypt was called the Pharaoh.

"I had a dream about seven cows," said the Pharaoh. "They were very nice, fat cows. Then seven thin and ugly cows came along and ate the nice fat ones."

Then the Pharaoh told about a second dream. "Seven bunches of grain were growing on one plant. They were strong, fat bunches of grain. Then seven thin and dried up bunches of grain came and ate up the seven fat ones."

"Tell me, Joseph," said the Pharaoh. "What do my dreams mean?"

"I'm not sure," said Joseph. "But God will help me understand what your dreams mean. Then I will tell you."

So Joseph asked God for help. Then he told the Pharaoh, "Both dreams mean the same thing. For seven years, all the plants and all the animals will grow very well in Egypt. There will be lots of food for everyone. In fact there will be more food than you can eat.

"After that, for seven years, there will be hardly any food. The plants and the animals will not grow because there won't be any rain. It will be a famine."

"Oh, dear!" said the Pharaoh. "What shall I do?"

"Find someone who will help people put food away during the seven years when everything is going very well," said

Joseph. "Then they will have enough to eat during the seven years when there isn't enough food."

"That's a good idea," said the Pharaoh. "And do you know who I am going to put in charge of all this?"

"No," said Joseph.

"You," said the Pharaoh. "I want you to go all over Egypt. I want you to ask people to put away some of the food during the seven good years. Then they will have enough to eat during the seven bad years."

The Pharaoh's dream came true, just as Joseph had said it would. For seven years, there seemed to be so much food, people didn't know what to do with it.

Then the seven years of famine came. Plants and animals died because there was no rain. People were so glad that Joseph had asked them to put some of the food away. Even though there was a famine, they had something to eat.

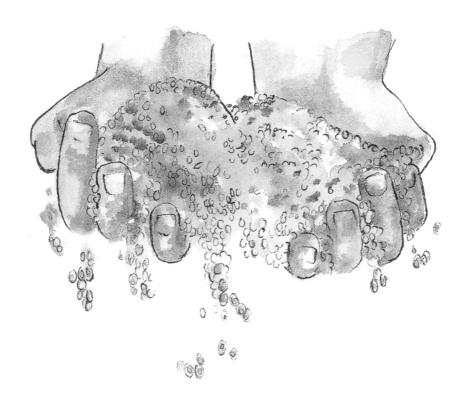

Joseph and His Brothers

Genesis 42 – 45

The famine was happening all over. Joseph and the people of Egypt had enough to eat. But in other countries, people were starving.

Far away in Canaan, Joseph's brothers and sisters and his father Jacob had hardly anything to eat.

One day Jacob said to his sons, "I hear there's lots of food in Egypt. Take some of the donkeys and go to Egypt to see if you can buy some."

So ten of the brothers left for Egypt. Benjamin didn't go because he was the youngest. His father worried that Benjamin might get hurt on such a long trip.

When the brothers got to Egypt, they asked, "Where can we buy food?"

"Go see the person who takes care of all the food," they were told.

Of course, the brothers didn't know that was Joseph. When they had sold Joseph to the traders many years before that, they didn't think they would ever see him again.

Joseph knew his brothers right away. Joseph was very surprised but he didn't say anything.

He was glad to see his brothers. But Joseph was still angry at them for selling him to the traders. Joseph felt both angry and happy. He was all mixed up inside.

"I think you are spies," Joseph said.

"Oh, no," said the brothers. "We're just ten brothers who have come to buy food. We're not spies."

"If you are brothers, what is your father's name?"

"Our father's name is Jacob. He is living in Canaan."

Joseph was so happy to hear that his father was still alive. He had to stop talking for a while, and he turned away from his brothers. He didn't want them to see the tears in his eyes.

"Are there other members of your family?" Joseph asked.

"There is one more brother, Benjamin. But he was too young to come with us."

"Any others?" Joseph was feeling angry now.

"Well, no. There was another brother, but he died."

"What do you mean, 'he died'?" Joseph was very angry.

The brothers just stood there. They didn't know what to say. They were afraid to say they had sold their brother as a slave.

Joseph could see from the faces of his brothers that they really were very sorry for what they had done.

"I am Joseph, your brother," he said.

The brothers couldn't believe it at first. It didn't seem possible. Then they felt afraid. "If this really is Joseph," they thought, "he will be very angry at us for what we did to him."

"Don't be afraid," said Joseph. "I think God wanted me to be in Egypt. God wanted me to help people so they wouldn't starve."

"Thank God," said Reuben, the oldest brother. "Thank God!"

Then the brothers started hugging Joseph and Joseph was hugging them and they were hugging each other. All of them were crying.

Finally Joseph blew his nose and said, "Go back to Canaan. Bring Father and Benjamin and the whole family here to Egypt. I know a nice place where you can live. And there's lots of food here in Egypt."

When the brothers had told Jacob for the twentieth time about Joseph in Egypt, the old man finally believed them. Suddenly he looked as if he was twenty years younger.

"Well," said Jacob. "What are we waiting for? Don't just stand around. Let's go."

As Jacob and all his family left Canaan, God came and repeated the promise. "Israel will become a great nation," said God. "And you will come back again to live in your own country."

That is how the people called "Israel" came to be living in Egypt.

The people of the house of Israel did not go back to Canaan. About 400 years had passed
since the time of Joseph. Over those years the people of Israel began to call themselves "Hebrews."
The Hebrews had kept on living in Egypt because they liked it there. There was lots of food.
But after 400 years most of the Hebrews had become slaves. They had to work for the
Egyptians. But there got to be more and more Hebrews. The Egyptians began to be afraid.

Miriam Saves Her Brother

Exodus 1 & 2

"Those Hebrews!" grumped the Pharaoh. "Soon there will be more Hebrews than Egyptians. Why doesn't somebody do something?"

"Sir," said one of the helpers. "You are the Pharaoh, the King of Egypt. Could you do something?"

"I guess so," said the Pharaoh. He talked to Shiphrah and Puah. They were midwives, women who help when mothers are having babies.

"When one of the Hebrew women has a baby boy," the Pharaoh said, "I want you to kill it."

Shiphrah and Puah could hardly believe that someone would ask for such a terrible thing. So they made a plan.

"Let's tell the Pharaoh how strong the Hebrew women are," said Puah. "Let's say they don't need us to help the babies be born."

"Their babies are born before we get there," Shiphrah told the Pharaoh.

This was a very brave thing for the two midwives to do. If Pharaoh had found out, he might have killed them. But the

Pharaoh believed what Shiphrah and Puah said.

So the Pharaoh tried something else. He gave an order: "When a boy baby is born, throw it in the river and drown it." The Pharaoh sent his soldiers to look in all the houses to make sure all the baby boys were drowned.

The Hebrew people tried everything to keep their babies away from the Pharaoh's soldiers. But usually the soldiers found the babies anyway.

When a woman named Jochebed gave birth to a baby boy, she and her husband Amram didn't know what to do. They kept the baby hidden for a while. But as the baby grew it was noisy sometimes. They knew the soldiers would find the baby and kill it.

One day Jochebed and the baby's older sister, Miriam, had an idea. They made a special basket for the baby. They fixed the basket so it would float on water.

Then Jochebed and Miriam took the basket to the edge of the river. They put the basket in the water among the reeds. "The soldiers will never find the baby here," said Jochebed. "Miriam, please stay close by so nothing bad happens to the baby."

Imagine Miriam's surprise when she saw a princess come down to the river. It was the Pharaoh's daughter coming to have a bath.

Now Miriam was really worried. "If the princess sees the basket with the baby, she'll call the soldiers. They will kill my baby brother."

Sure enough, the princess saw the basket. She sent one of her helpers to get it for her.

"Oh, what a beautiful baby," said the princess. The little baby was crying, so the princess picked it up and cuddled it. "I'm going to take care of this baby as if he were my very own."

When Miriam heard that, she had another good idea. She ran over to the princess and said, "Would you like me to find someone who can feed the baby milk from her breasts and take very good care of it for you?"

"Why, yes!" said the princess.

So Miriam ran and got Jochebed, her mother.

"Take this baby, and take good care of him," the princess told Jochebed. "I will pay you for your work."

Later in the day, Miriam and her mother were talking about what had happened. Miriam jumped up and down and just squealed, she was so happy.

"Shhh," said her mother. "People will hear you." But Jochebed couldn't keep from laughing. "All I wanted was to keep my baby from being killed by the Pharaoh. Now the Pharaoh's daughter is paying me to look after my own little baby. I think God must have some plans for this child."

When the baby got a little older, the princess took the baby to the palace to live.

"I will raise him as if he is an Egyptian," said the princess. "He will live like a prince in the Pharaoh's palace. And I will call him Moses, which means, 'I drew him out of the water.'"

Moses Kills a Man

Exodus 2:11-25

Moses liked living in the Pharaoh's palace, most of the time. But sometimes, somebody in the palace got angry at him. Or the princess got annoyed. Then they called him a "Hebrew."

As he grew older, Moses realized that Hebrews were people who worked as slaves for the Pharaoh. The Egyptians usually treated the Hebrews like animals.

As Moses grew up, he really wanted to learn more about the Hebrews. "They are my people," he said to himself. Moses even wanted to find out who his real mom and dad were. He could barely remember them.

It didn't take Moses long to find his family. He had some wonderful evenings talking with his mother Jochebed, his sister Miriam, his father Amram, and his brother Aaron.

They told Moses about the brave midwives. They told him how they made a basket for him to float on the water. They told how Pharaoh's daughter found him. They laughed about how Miriam offered to find someone to look after the baby.

They also told Moses about an old, old promise that God had made to the Hebrew people. They told Moses about Abraham and Sarah, about Isaac and Leah and Rachel, and about Joseph and his brothers.

Moses felt very mixed up sometimes. "I live like a prince in a palace," he thought. "The princess treats me like a son. But my people are slaves! Who am I, anyway?"

Moses often went to the places where the Hebrews worked. They had to make big buildings for the Pharaoh. Moses noticed that the Hebrews didn't have enough food to eat. Their bodies were covered with sores.

Sometimes the Hebrews were too sick to work. Then the bosses would beat them with whips. Moses felt angry.

One day Moses saw one of the bosses beating a worker who could hardly stand up. "Please don't hit me any more," cried the worker. "I just can't stand up. My legs hurt so much."

"You're just lazy," yelled the boss beating the worker some more. "Get up and get to work!"

Moses got very angry. He hit the boss hard and killed him.

Moses knew he was in trouble. He ran away out of the city and into the hills. He ran all the way to a place called Midian.

Moses felt tired. When he came to a well, he had a big drink of cold water and sat down to rest. While he sat there, seven sisters came by. They began giving their flock of sheep a drink.

Just then, other shepherds came along and chased the seven sisters away. Moses got angry again. "The seven sisters were here first!" yelled Moses.

The sisters wanted to say "thank you" to Moses. They invited him to come for supper. As it turned out, Moses got along very well with the seven sisters, and with their mother and father. They asked Moses to stay with them.

After a while Moses and one of the seven sisters got married. Some time later, Zipporah and Moses had a baby.

Moses was very happy with his new family. But even so, he remembered his home in Egypt. He thought about his own Hebrew people. Moses worried about how the Pharaoh was treating them.

Most of all, he thought about his mother Jochebed and his sister Miriam. Moses thought about the princess who had adopted him. He thought about the midwives who wouldn't kill the babies, even though the Pharaoh told them to.

"Those women must really have been living in God's way," he thought. "If it hadn't been for them, I wouldn't be alive."

Moses Goes
Back to Egypt

Exodus 3 & 4

Back in Egypt, things were
worse for the Hebrews. The
Pharaoh who wanted to kill Moses had died.
The new Pharaoh made the Hebrews work even harder.
Moses often thought about them.

One day, out in the hills, Moses saw something very strange.
It was a bush on fire. Moses didn't know why a bush should be
burning all by itself out there in the hills.

Moses went a little closer. He saw that even though the bush
was on fire, it wasn't getting burned up. The bush just kept
burning and burning. "I'd better go even closer to see this,"
said Moses.

Then Moses heard a voice. "Moses! Moses!"

Moses was afraid. "Yes?" he said. "Here I am."

"Don't come any closer, Moses," said the voice. "And take
off your shoes. You are standing on holy ground."

Moses was even more afraid now. He didn't run away, but
he took off his shoes quickly. "Maybe it's God talking to
me," he thought.

"I am the God
of your great, great,
grandparents," said
the voice. "I am the

God who gave the promise to Abraham and Sarah. I am the God of Isaac and Rebecca."

Moses covered his face with his hands. Now he was very afraid.

"Moses," the voice said, "I have heard the cry of the Hebrew people in Egypt. I know how much they are hurting. I want to take them out of Egypt and send them back to the land they came from, in Canaan. And Moses, I am sending you to lead them out of Egypt."

"Yes but, God," said Moses, "I don't know how to do that."

"I will be with you, Moses. I will help you."

"Yes but," said Moses, "what if they ask me your name? What should I tell them?"

"Moses," said God. "I am who I am. If they want to know who sent you, say 'I AM' sent you."

"Yes but," Moses said again, "I don't know how to talk very well. When I try to say things, my words get all mixed up. Can't you send somebody else?"

"*Moses*! No more 'yes-buts.'" God seemed to be getting angry at Moses. "If you need someone to talk for you, ask your brother Aaron. Aaron is already on his way to meet you, to ask you to help your people. Just remember. I will be with you. Now *go*!"

Moses didn't want to go. He was afraid to go.

But Moses went. Moses believed that God would be with him.

Moses and his wife Zipporah and their baby began the long walk back to Egypt. Along the way, sure enough, his brother Aaron was coming toward him. They gave each other a hug and a kiss and sat down to talk.

"Pharaoh is making our people work harder," said Aaron. "They don't have enough food. Many of them are sick."

Moses told Aaron about the burning bush, and about what God had told him to do.

So Moses and Aaron went back to Egypt. They had a big meeting with all the Hebrew people.

"God really cares about how much you are hurting," said Aaron to all the people. "And God will help us get away from Pharaoh."

The Hebrews Leave Egypt

Exodus 5 – 12

The Hebrews all cheered when Moses and Aaron spoke to them. They hated being slaves. They wanted to be free.

So the brothers went to the palace to talk to Pharaoh.

"God wants you to let our people go," they said.

Pharaoh was very angry. "I will not let your people go. They belong to me. Tell your people to get back to work."

Pharaoh was so angry, he made things even harder for the Hebrew slaves. The Hebrews had to make bricks for Pharaoh's big buildings. They made the bricks out of clay and straw.

Now Pharaoh told them. "You have to get your own straw. Go out into the fields to find it. But you have to make just as many bricks as before." Then Pharaoh told his bosses to beat the people if they didn't make enough bricks.

Then the Hebrew people were angry at Moses and Aaron.

"You ask Pharaoh to let us go. What happens? We have to work harder. You make things worse. Why don't you just go away and mind your own business?"

Moses was upset. "Is this why you sent me here?" he said to God. "Now Pharaoh makes people work harder. You made things worse!"

"Moses," God said. "I made a promise to Abraham and Sarah and all their children's children. I made a promise that you will be a great nation. Go and tell that to my people."

So Moses talked to the Hebrews. "Remember God's promise," he said. "Please trust God. It's very important."

Some of the people believed Moses. Others didn't.

God helped Moses and Aaron try to make Pharaoh let the people go. God turned the river into blood. Zillions of frogs and bugs and flies came. The cows and sheep got sick and there were sores on the people. There was hail and grasshoppers. One time it turned dark in the middle of the day. These things only happened to the Egyptians, not the Hebrews.

But Pharaoh would not let the Hebrew people go.

Then God said to Moses and Aaron. "I will do one more thing to Pharaoh and to the Egyptians. Then they will let my people go."

So God told Moses exactly what was going to happen. Moses had to explain it to the Hebrew people.

"Listen carefully," Moses said. "I want you all to get ready. We are going to leave Egypt. But tonight, I want you to have a very special meal.

"Kill a small goat or a sheep, and roast it. Take some of the blood from the goat or sheep. Smear it on your front door. That way God will know which houses are Hebrew and which are Egyptian."

That night the Hebrew people ate the roasted sheep. They smeared the blood on their front doors. Many of the people said prayers to God.

God made a sickness come into the homes of all the Egyptians. The oldest child in every house died. Even the Pharaoh's oldest child died.

But none of the Hebrew children died. And the Hebrews said, "The sickness *passed over* our homes because we had put the blood on our doors."

That same night all the Egyptians, especially Pharaoh, wanted the Hebrews to leave. "Get out," they yelled. "Get out quickly. Take anything you want, just go."

The Hebrew people left quickly.

It was like a whole city full of people all walking out together. Many of them had started making bread. They had to leave so quickly, they didn't have time to let the bread get soft. They picked everything up and left.

Miriam was walking with her two brothers, Moses and Aaron. "We will never forget this time," she said to them. "My people will always remember how God was with us. We will never forget God's promise."

"We will never forget," said Moses.

And the Hebrew people still remember this time every year. They remember what God did for them many, many years ago.

They celebrate with a special meal. They tell the story of how the Hebrew people were freed from being slaves. They eat food like hard bread that reminds them of what happened.

They call that celebration "Passover" because they remember how the terrible sickness passed over their homes and their children.

A Long, Long Journey

Exodus 14 & 15

Miriam and her brothers and all the Hebrew people began a long, long journey. It was a journey that would last for forty years. Many things happened to them on this journey.

The first thing was that Pharaoh changed his mind. Again.

The Hebrew people were camping beside the sea. They didn't know how to get to the other side. Then off in the distance, someone saw Pharaoh's soldiers coming. Hundreds of them, with their horses and their sharp swords.

"What are we going to do?" the people said to Moses. "Did you have to drag us all the way out here in the desert? You've made things worse again. Now Pharaoh's soldiers will kill us."

Once again, God saved the Hebrews. A strong wind blew the water away so the Hebrews could walk through to the other side of the sea. They had to walk fast because Pharaoh's army was right behind them. When all the Hebrews were on the other side, the wind stopped. The water came back. Pharaoh's soldiers drowned.

When all the Hebrew people were safe again, they decided to have a celebration. A party. They wanted to say "thank you" to God for saving them.

Moses and the people sang a long song.

Then Miriam gathered all the women together. Miriam was a prophet. A prophet is a leader who helps people understand how to live in God's way.

Miriam beat her little drum. She and all the women danced. It was a happy dance. And Miriam sang a song.

Sing a song to God
For God has done great things.
God has thrown the horse and rider
In the sea.

Then everybody joined in the dancing and singing.

"We're not slaves any more," they shouted. "We are free! Thank you, God!"

Special Food

Exodus 16 – 17:7

"It's such a long way,"
Miriam sighed.
"I know," said Aaron.
"It's hot in the daytime and cold at night. And I'm so hungry."

"So am I," said Miriam. "But there's nothing to eat."

The Hebrew people hadn't eaten anything for days. "Why did you drag us into the desert to die?" they said to Moses. "We were slaves in Egypt, but we had enough to eat. Now we are not slaves but we are so hungry. You've made things worse again."

"Believe me," said Moses. "God got us out of Egypt. God will give us food."

Sure enough, in the evening, a whole flock of birds flew into their camp. The people caught them and cooked them for food.

The next morning they found some white sticky stuff growing on the plants and on the ground. They called it manna.

"Hmmm! This is good," said Miriam.

"What does it taste like?" asked Aaron.

"Sort of like a biscuit made with honey. I like it."

Moses told the people the manna would come every day. "This is God's bread," he said. "Gather just enough for one day. Except on the sixth day, gather twice as much. Because the seventh day is our Sabbath, a day of rest. Gather enough for the Sabbath on the sixth day so you can rest on the seventh."

Now the people had enough to eat, but they were thirsty. There was no water anywhere. They started complaining again.

"Did you have to drag us out of Egypt just so we would die of thirst here in the desert?" they yelled at Moses. "You've made things worse again!"

So Moses asked God. "What am I supposed to do? They are ready to kill me."

God told Moses to walk out into the desert. "Go to a special rock that I'll show you. Hit it hard with your walking stick."

Moses did what God told him to do. Clean, pure water came running out of the rock.

Then Moses said to the people, "God is with us. Remember that. God is with us. We are God's people!"

But the people didn't always remember. It's hard to remember that God cares about you, when you are hungry and thirsty and tired and hot and homesick.

The Ten Commandments

Exodus 19 & 20

Three months after God helped the Hebrew people get away
from Egypt, they came to a place called Sinai. There was a high
mountain in Sinai.

One day God asked Moses to come up the mountain.

"I want to give you a message for the people of Israel," God
said to Moses. "Remember how I brought you out of Egypt?
I carried you out like a mother eagle carries her babies.
Remember the promises I made to your great, great, great
grandparents? I promised that you would be a great nation. I
promised that many years from now people would learn about
me because of you. But you must do the things I ask you to do."

So Moses went back and told all the people to gather near the
mountain. "God has some very important things to tell us, and
we have to be ready to listen carefully. Don't try to come up the
mountain with me. Just wait at the bottom. You will be able to
hear God's voice."

So the people gathered near the mountain. At the top of the
mountain they could see smoke and fire. They could hear
thunder. Everything shook like an earthquake.

Moses went up the mountain, into the smoke and the fire. There God told him ten important things to remember. We call them The Ten Commandments.

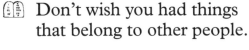 I am your God. I brought you out of Egypt, out of the land of slavery. Don't pretend there are any other gods. I am the only one.

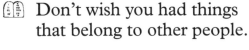 Don't make pictures or statues or anything else that you think might look like me. Don't bow down to them or pray to them.

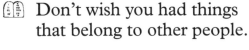 Be careful how you use my name. When you speak my name, you must mean what you are saying.

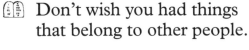 Remember the Sabbath day, the seventh day of the week. Work on the other six days. Rest on the seventh day and make it a special day.

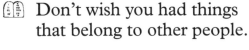 Treat your mother and your father with respect. Be good to them.

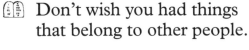 Don't kill anyone.

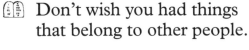 Don't have sex with anyone you are not married to.

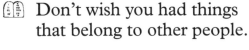 Don't steal.

 Don't tell lies about anyone.

 Don't wish you had things that belong to other people.

The people were afraid when they saw all the smoke and heard God's voice. But they said "thank you" to God. They were glad to know how to live in God's way.

Moses Sees the New Land

Deuteronomy 34

Moses stood up on top of Mount Nebo. From there, he could see the land of Canaan. This was the land that God had promised the Hebrew people.

Moses felt sad and happy. He was sad and happy as he thought about all the things that had happened in his life.

Moses remembered how God had spoken to him from a burning bush. God told Moses to go and lead the people out of Egypt. Moses remembered how God had kept them in the desert for forty years.

The desert had been like a school. God had wanted the Hebrew people to know what it meant to be God's chosen people, God's special people. That's why God had given them the ten commandments and many other lessons about how to live in God's way.

Moses was sad. The Hebrews had found it so hard to trust God. They found it hard to believe that God would be with them even when bad things were happening to them. But Moses was happy. Now, at last, the Hebrews were ready to go into the land God had promised.

It looked like such a beautiful land from there on top of Mount Nebo. That made Moses happy. It would be good for the Hebrew people to get out of the hot, dry desert. But Moses felt sad. God had said to Moses, "I will let you see this new land with your eyes, but you can't go into it."

Moses was 120 years old. He was still strong and healthy, but he knew he would die soon.

So Moses asked one of his helpers, Joshua, to stand beside him. "People of Israel," said Moses. "Joshua has God's spirit in him. I am going to die soon. God has asked Joshua to be your leader."

Then Moses put his hand on Joshua's head, and said a prayer to God. "Please God, help Joshua be a good leader. Help him to listen to all the things you say."

Not long after that, Moses died. The people of Israel were very sad.

Since then, the people of Israel have never had a leader like Moses. They all said it was because Moses was the only one who talked to God face to face.

The People
Claim the Promised Land

Joshua 1, 3 & 4

Joshua was a little bit afraid. He didn't know if he could be as good a leader as Moses.

But God said to Joshua, "Don't be afraid. I will help you feel strong. I want you to lead the people into the Promised Land so that my promise to Abraham and Sarah can come true. I will be with you wherever you go."

So Joshua led all the Hebrews down out of the desert into a land called Canaan. It had been a long journey through the desert from Egypt. Now at last the Hebrew people were in the land God had promised to them.

To get into Canaan, the Hebrews had to cross the river Jordan. "How will we get across?" they wondered. But as soon as their feet touched the water, the river got dry.

Everyone was surprised. "God did this for us," said Joshua.

"God has helped us again. We must do something to remember this."

The Hebrews were divided into twelve very large families. These families had aunts and uncles and cousins and second cousins. These big families were called "tribes." Sometimes there were hundreds of people in a tribe.

"Let the leader of each tribe find a big stone from the middle of the river. Bring each stone up to the other side of the river. From now on, whenever people see these stones, they will remember what God has done for us."

When the Hebrews had all crossed the river, the water started flowing again.

So they said "thank you" to God in a very special way. They had a Passover meal with some special food. It was their first meal with food from the new country, Canaan. The Hebrews remembered how God had brought them out of Egypt. They remembered the promise God made to Abraham and Sarah.

"Thank you God," said Joshua. "You got us out of Egypt. You took care of us in the desert. Now we are in a new country. We're not slaves any more. We are free."

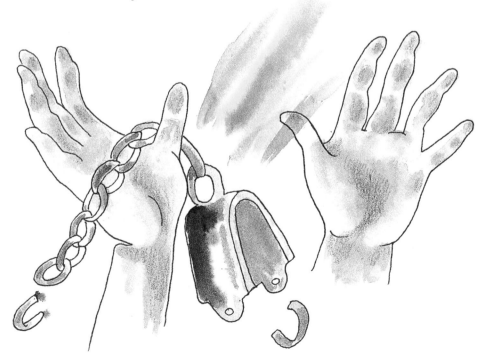

Not all the stories in the Bible are happy stories. The Hebrews sometimes thought God wanted them to fight wars. They thought God wanted them to kill people. Many people don't think God is like that. Many people feel God loves everybody, and that God is sad when people are fighting.

The Battle of Jericho

Joshua 2, 5:13 – 6:27

The Hebrews fought many wars in Canaan. The people who already lived in Canaan didn't want the Hebrews to take their land. One of the big cities in Canaan was Jericho.

The Hebrews were helped by a woman named Rahab.

Joshua's spies had come to Jericho to see how they could attack it. Rahab let them into her house, because she had heard about the Hebrew people and how they had beaten other people in their wars.

"The people of Jericho are very afraid of you," Rahab told the spies.

Some of the people of Jericho saw the spies go into Rahab's house and came to capture them. Rahab hid the spies under some straw.

"Thank you Rahab," said the spies. "When we start fighting with the people of Jericho, we promise not to hurt you or your family. But we need a secret signal so the soldiers will know which is your house.

"I have a bright red rope," said Rahab. "I'll hang it outside of my window. Then the soldiers will know."

Joshua's spies went back to their camp. "There are thick walls all around Jericho," they said. "We need a special plan to break those walls down."

This is what the Hebrews did.

The first day the Hebrews walked around the city once. "Shhh," said Joshua. "Be very quiet. Don't say anything. Just let some of the people blow on their horns." The people of Jericho wondered. "Why are they doing that?"

The second day the Hebrews walked around the city again. "Shhh," said Joshua. "Don't talk. Just blow on the horns." The people of Jericho wondered. "Why are they doing that?"

The Hebrews did the same thing on the third day. And on the fourth day. And on the fifth day. And on the sixth day. "Shhh," said Joshua. "Don't talk. Just blow on the horns." The people of Jericho wondered. "Why are they doing that?"

On the seventh day, they walked around the city once. "Shhh," said Joshua. "Don't talk. Just blow on the horns." The people of Jericho wondered. "Why are they doing that?"

They walked around again. Then again. And again. And again. And again. "Shhh," said Joshua. "Don't talk. Just blow on the horns." The people of Jericho wondered. "Why are they doing that?"

The seventh time, Joshua suddenly gave the signal. Everyone shouted as loud as they could. The horn players blew really hard. It was a terrible noise. It sounded like a big earthquake. Suddenly, the walls around Jericho came tumbling down.

Then there was a big fight between the Hebrews and the people of Jericho. "Look," said Joshua. "There's Rahab's red rope. Remember how she helped us."

The Hebrews Remember

Joshua 9, 24:24-29

Bit by bit, the Hebrew people began to live in many parts of Canaan. It was a nice place. They believed God had given it to them.

The Hebrews didn't have to fight for all of Canaan, the way they did for Jericho. Sometimes they just moved in near the people who already lived there.

Some of the people who lived in Canaan came and said to the Hebrews, "We live very far away. And we are very poor. Promise you won't attack us."

"We promise," said the Hebrews.

Then the Hebrews found out these people didn't live far away, and they were not poor. So they said, "You tricked us!"

"Yes," said the people of Canaan, "but you promised not to attack us."

"We won't attack you," said the Hebrews, "but because you tricked us, you have to carry our water and get wood for our fires. You have to work for us. You will have to be like slaves to us."

The Hebrew people had already forgotten how awful it was to be slaves.

Sometimes they forgot how God had brought them out of Egypt where they had been slaves.

More and more, the Hebrews began to find places to live in the land of Canaan. Joshua was still their leader, but he was getting very old. He wondered if the Hebrews would remember to live in God's way.

Joshua asked all the people to come together in one place. He set a big rock up on its end and said, "This rock will remind us. It will remind our children. And our children's children."

Then Joshua said to the Hebrews, "Remember the promise God made to Abraham and Sarah. God has kept that promise, and now we have a land of our own to live in. Now we must keep our part of the promise."

Then the people said to Joshua, "We will remember to live in God's way."

"Are you sure?" asked Joshua.

"Yes," said the people. "We will try our very best."

Soon after that Joshua died. The people were very sad. Joshua had been a good leader.

The people of Israel began to live all over the land of Canaan. Usually they called themselves "Hebrews." They remembered the story of God's promise; God's covenant. They remembered what happened to Jacob. Then they called themselves "the people of Israel."

But often they forgot the story. The Hebrews forgot the promise they had made to God when Joshua died.

Many other people lived in Canaan too. Sometimes one group of people tried to be the boss over other groups, and then there would be fighting. Many people were hurt or killed.

Most of the people who lived in Canaan had kings and queens to tell them what to do. But not the people of Israel.

Whenever the Hebrews were in trouble, God would send a leader to help them. They called these leaders "judges." They weren't judges who sat in a court. They were leaders who helped the Hebrew people when there was an argument about something. Sometimes they were prophets. Prophets are people who love God very much and help others understand what God wants them to do. Sometimes the judges were like generals of an army. One of the strongest and best judges was Deborah.

A Mother for Israel

Judges 4 & 5

The people of Israel were in trouble. They had been fighting with the King of Canaan. They lost the fight. Now the King of Canaan was hurting them.

Deborah was a prophet. She was a strong, wise leader who helped people understand how to live in God's way.

When one of the Hebrews was having an argument with another Hebrew, they would both come to Deborah. "Please help us decide what to do."

Many of the Hebrew people came to Deborah to tell her about the cruel things the King of Canaan was doing. Finally, Deborah said, "We will get some people together and fight the King of Canaan."

Deborah thought that Barak would be a good leader for the army. So she sent him a letter and said, "Please come to see me."

When Barak came to Deborah, she said, "Get ten thousand people together. Go and fight the King of Canaan."

Barak said to her, "I'm afraid to go by myself. If you go with me, I will go to fight the King."

The Hebrews who were going to fight the King were afraid. Deborah helped them to feel brave and strong. "Deborah is our leader. She is like a strong mother in Israel," the Hebrews said. "She helps us feel we can do important things."

Barak and the Hebrews were able to beat the King of Canaan, and so they were free again.

Then Deborah and Barak sang a song together. Some of the words went like this:

> We had terrible days in our country,
> A very hard time in our land.
> In the small towns, nothing could happen,
> No one could travel the roads.
> A strong mother arose in Israel,
> A leader whose name was Deborah.
> Deborah helped us remember,
> Remember the promise of God.

The story of Samson and Delilah is also in the Book of Judges. But Samson wasn't famous for being a wise and helpful judge the way Deborah was. Samson was famous for being very strong.

Samson and Delilah

Judges 16

Samson was a Hebrew. He was in love with Delilah, who was a Philistine. The Philistines were the people who lived in Canaan when the Hebrews came from Egypt. They often fought with each other.

The Philistines really hated Samson because he had killed many of their people. So they talked to Delilah.

"Help us find out why Samson is so strong," they said. "If we can find his secret, then maybe we can capture him. We'll give you a lot of money."

Samson did whatever he wanted. He was so strong. He often hurt people. Everyone was afraid of Samson.

Delilah asked Samson. "Tell me, what makes you so strong?"

So Samson teased her. "Tie me up with new bow strings, or new ropes. Then I won't be strong any more."

Delilah tied him up with new ropes. Samson broke them like soggy spaghetti.

Delilah asked and asked until finally Samson told her. "I am strong because of my long hair. If I didn't have long hair, I wouldn't be strong any more."

Delilah thought, "This must be the right answer. Samson is so proud of his long hair." Samson had seven braids in his hair. He had promised God never, ever to cut his hair.

While Samson was sleeping, Delilah asked a man to come in and cut off his long hair.

"Wake up Samson," Delilah called. Then she called the Philistines who were waiting outside. "Come and get him," she said. "He's as weak as a baby."

Samson tried to fight the Philistines. But they tied him up as easily as if he were a young child. Then the Philistines hurt his eyes so he couldn't see. And they locked Samson into a dark room all by himself.

When the Philistines had a party, they brought Samson out of his room. They laughed at him and teased him. "Show us how strong you are, Samson. See if you can lift a blade of grass all by yourself."

This happened many times. The Philistines forgot that Samson's hair was growing back in. He was still blind, but little by little he became strong again.

One day the Philistines had a big party with lots of people. They brought Samson in so they could tease him.

The Philistines tied Samson between two posts that held up the big house they were in. They teased him. "Big strong Samson. Show us how strong you are!"

Samson was very angry at the Philistines. "God," he said. "Make me strong just one more time. Please!" Then Samson pushed hard on the two posts that held up the house.

Crack! The posts broke and the house fell down on the Philistines and on Samson.

They were all killed. Samson too.

The Hebrews sometimes thought they were the only people in the whole world that God loved. They even had laws that said Hebrews couldn't marry anyone except another Hebrew.

Not all the Hebrews felt this way. Some felt God loved everybody, not just Hebrews. To show this, they liked to tell the story of Ruth and Naomi.

Ruth was not a Hebrew. But she became the grandmother of the greatest king the Hebrews ever had.

Two Brave Women

Ruth

Naomi was happy living in Bethlehem. She loved her husband and her two sons. But one year, a famine hit Bethlehem. A famine is when grain and vegetables won't grow because there is not enough rain. Sometimes Naomi and her family had nothing to eat for many days.

One day the four of them sat down to talk about their problem. Naomi's husband said, "I've heard they have lots of food in Moab."

"Isn't that very far away?" asked Naomi.

"Yes it is," said her husband. "But the people there are kind to the Hebrews. Maybe they would be kind to us."

"Let's go," said Naomi.

Things went well in Moab. Naomi and her family had enough to eat and people were kind to them.

In fact, Naomi's two sons got married in Moab. Naomi didn't like it at first. She worried about the Hebrew law that said Hebrews should only marry other Hebrews.

"But Ruth and Orpah are such fine people," Naomi thought. "How can it be wrong for my sons to marry them? They are just like daughters to me."

Then sad things happened. First Naomi's husband died. Soon after that, her two sons died.

Naomi and Ruth and Orpah cried together. It wasn't just that they were very sad about their husbands. In those days women who didn't have husbands might starve. The husbands were the only ones who could get money for food. A woman without a husband might have no place to live. Sometimes these women died.

Life was hardest for Naomi. She had no cousins or aunts or uncles in Moab to help her.

Finally, Naomi said to Ruth and Orpah, "I have to go back home to Bethlehem. I have some cousins there who may help me. And I have heard that the famine is over and the people of Bethlehem have food again. I think you should go back and live with your mothers."

Orpah said, "Yes, I'll go back to live with my mother."

But not Ruth.

"I love you more than anyone, Naomi," she said.

"You would be unhappy in Bethlehem," said Naomi. "You have no friends or family there."

"Please don't ask me to leave you," said Ruth, "or to keep from following after you. For where you go, I will go. Where you live, I will live. Your people will be my people, and your God will be my God."

Naomi gave Ruth a very big hug. "I say 'thank you' to God so often for you, Ruth. I don't want to go away from you either."

"Then let's go to Bethlehem together," said Ruth.

They were still very poor in Bethlehem. Ruth picked up little bits of grain that were left behind in the fields. It was very hard work in the hot sun all day. Ruth felt tired and her back hurt when she got home at night. Naomi worried that Ruth might work too hard and get sick.

Ruth was gathering leftover bits of grain in a field that belonged to Boaz. Boaz was Naomi's cousin. He had heard about Ruth and how she had been so kind and loving to Naomi.

Soon Ruth and Boaz got to know each other and to love each other. They got married, and Naomi went to live with them.

"Look at that," some of the neighbors said. "Boaz is marrying Ruth and she isn't a Hebrew. That's awful."

"It's not awful," said Boaz. "It's wonderful. Ruth is a good, kind person."

Naomi had always wanted to be a grandmother, but her two sons had died before there were any babies. Now Naomi began

to hope again. Maybe Ruth and Boaz would have a baby.

They did. And all of Naomi's friends in Bethlehem came to see her new grandchild.

Ruth and Boaz named the baby Obed. He became the grandfather of King David.

King David became Israel's most famous king.

Hannah Prays for a Baby

1 Samuel 1& 2

Hannah and Elkanah were unhappy. They loved each other very much. But they wanted to have a baby. Now they were getting older. They worried that they might never have a child.

One day Hannah went to God's house in Shiloh. Hannah prayed to God that she could have a baby.

She prayed for a long, long time. Her lips moved as she talked to God in her mind. And Hannah's body swayed back and forth as she prayed.

Eli was an old man who lived and worked in God's house at Shiloh. He watched Hannah as she prayed. He thought she was acting strangely.

"Have you been drinking too much wine?" Eli asked Hannah.

"Oh, no!" said Hannah. "I haven't had any wine or beer. I was praying to God to give me a baby."

Eli knew that Hannah had been praying to God. "I hope God will give you a baby," said Eli with a big smile.

Hannah went back to her home. A few months later, it happened. Hannah was so happy when she realized she was pregnant. "Elkanah!" she shouted. "Elkanah! We're going to have a baby!" Hannah sang and danced and said, "Thank you, God!" over and over.

They named the baby Samuel which means, "We asked God for him."

"This baby is a special gift from God," she said to Elkanah when the baby was born. "I would like Samuel to be God's helper all the time."

Little Samuel grew quickly. Soon he was almost three years old and didn't need to have milk from his mother's breasts any more. Then Hannah took him to God's house in Shiloh.

"I want Samuel to live here with you," she said to old Eli. "You can teach him how to be God's special helper. I'll bring him new clothes and other things that he needs."

Eli was very happy, but he didn't know what to say.

Hannah knew what to say. She said, "Thank you, God!" And she sang all the way home.

God Calls Samuel

1 Samuel 3

Samuel was very young when his mother, Hannah, took him to
live with Eli in God's house.

Samuel tried very hard to be a good helper to old Eli. Eli was
getting very old. He couldn't see very well. Samuel ran to get
things for Eli. He helped Eli with his clothes and with his food.

It was hard work for Samuel because he was just a
young boy.

One night, Samuel helped old Eli get ready for bed.
Then Samuel went to bed himself. He felt tired after helping
Eli all day.

As Samuel was drifting off to sleep, he thought he heard
someone call his name. "Samuel! Samuel!" He jumped up and
ran to Eli.

"Did you call me?" Samuel asked.

"No, I didn't call you," said Eli. "Go back to bed."

So Samuel went back to bed. But he couldn't sleep. Then
he heard it again. This time Samuel was sure it was a voice
calling his name.

"Samuel! Samuel!" Again, Samuel ran to Eli.

"No, I didn't call you," said Eli. "Go back to sleep."

This time, Samuel was really wide awake. Again he heard
the same voice calling "Samuel! Samuel!" Since there was no
one around except himself and Eli, he thought it *had* to be Eli.

Again, he ran to Eli.

"No. I didn't call you," said old Eli. By now Eli was wide awake too.

"Samuel," said Eli. "I think maybe God is trying to talk to you. Next time you hear your name called say, 'Here I am. Your servant is listening.'"

Samuel lay on his bed waiting. There was no light except the moon shining in his small window. He felt a little bit afraid.

"What would God want to say to me?" Samuel wondered. "Does God speak to children? Shouldn't God wait till I'm grown up?"

Then Samuel heard the voice again. "Samuel! Samuel!"

"Here I am," said Samuel. "Your servant is listening."

Then God told Samuel some things Samuel didn't really want to hear. "Eli is a good person, but he wasn't a good father to his sons," said God. "When Eli's sons were doing evil things, Eli didn't tell them to stop. So I am going to punish Eli's whole family. Eli's sons will not be able to live in God's house the way Eli did."

The next morning, Samuel tried to stay away from Eli. Samuel didn't want to tell Eli what God had said. But Eli called to him.

"Come and tell me what God said to you," said Eli. "Tell me everything."

So Samuel told Eli. Samuel cried because he could see the hurt look in his old friend's eyes.

"It's all right," said Eli when he saw Samuel crying. "God is right. Let God do whatever is the right thing."

Samuel talked with God a lot after that. As he grew older, people began to know that he was God's prophet. A prophet is someone who helps people understand how God wants them to live.

People came from many places to talk to Samuel and hear what he would tell them about God. Samuel helped many people learn to live in God's way.

David and Goliath

*1 Samuel 17, with portions from
Chapters 16, 18 & 19.*

David lived in the town of Bethlehem. He liked to hear stories
about his great grandmother Ruth. Ruth had come from a
faraway country to live in Bethlehem.

David was a shepherd. Each day he took the sheep that
belonged to his family, and helped the sheep find grass to eat.

David liked to sit on the hillsides as he looked after the
sheep. Sometimes he made up songs about the sheep, the hills,
and God.

Sometimes looking after the sheep was easy. Sometimes it
could be hard and dangerous. If one of the sheep got lost,
David had to find it. If lions and wolves attacked the sheep,
David had to chase them away.

David used a sling to fight the lions and wolves. The sling
was two strong pieces of string, with a patch of leather in
between. David put a small stone in the patch of leather and
whirled it around his head. When he let go of one string, the
stone flew out, going very fast.

David practiced hard until he could hit anything. David
used the sling to protect his family's sheep against wild animals.

One day David's father, Jesse, came to David, "Your older
brothers are helping King Saul fight in a war," he said. "I want
you to take some food to them."

So David took the food and walked to where his brothers
were. He found that his brothers and all the other soldiers were
very afraid.

"We are fighting against the Philistines," they said. They pointed to the other side of the valley where the Philistine army was waiting to fight.

"One of the Philistines is a very big man named Goliath. Every morning he comes out and yells at us. 'Choose one of your men who is brave enough to fight me. If your man wins the fight, then you will win the war. If I win the fight, then the Philistines will win the war.'"

The next morning, David saw Goliath come out and yell at the Hebrew army. Goliath had a big spear in his hand and he looked very fierce.

So David said to King Saul. "Let me go and fight Goliath."

"But you're just a boy," said King Saul. "How can you fight such a big man?"

"I can fight lions and wolves to protect my sheep," David replied. "I can beat Goliath. God will take care of me."

David picked up some nice smooth, round stones. He put one of the stones in his sling.

David ran toward to Goliath. Goliath laughed when he saw a boy coming up to fight him. But David wasn't afraid. "You come at me with a sharp spear," David called to Goliath. "But I come to you with the help of God."

David whirled the sling around his head. Out flew a stone that hit Goliath right on the head. Goliath fell down dead.

"We won the war!" shouted all the Hebrew soldiers. Then they chased the Philistines away. And everybody said, "Hooray for David! He saved us from the Philistines."

David and Jonathan

1 Samuel 18 – 20

King Saul had asked
David to come and live
in the palace. Saul
liked David because he
was brave and strong,
and because David
could play wonderful
music on the harp.

David became very good friends with Jonathan, King Saul's
son. Jonathan and David liked to go for walks, to play games
and just talk. Even as they grew to be men, they were still
best friends.

King Saul had a kind of sickness that made him feel very
sad sometimes. When that happened, David played music for
the King. David liked to play on his harp and to sing songs for
the King. Then the King stopped feeling sad.

But then the King's sickness got worse. Not even David's
songs made the King feel better. Sometimes the King threw
things at everybody. Once he threw his spear at David. David
jumped away quickly. The King's spear might have killed him.

Jonathan talked to his father and tried to make the King not
feel so angry at everyone. That helped for a while, but King
Saul's sickness kept getting worse. The sickness made Saul feel
people liked David better than him. So Saul tried to kill David.

David ran away and hid. Jonathan came to help him.

"I will talk to my father again," said Jonathan. "He doesn't
really want to kill you, David."

"Yes, I think he does," said David. "And he won't listen to you anyway because he knows we are best friends."

"Let me try again," said Jonathan. "You hide in the field. I will talk to my father. Then I will come and tell you."

"That will be dangerous," said David. "Your father might find out and hurt you."

"I'll send a secret message," said Jonathan. "I'll come out to the field and pretend I'm practising with my bow and arrow. I'll bring a helper to chase my arrows. If I say to my helper, 'The arrows are farther away,' you'll know my father is still angry."

When Jonathan came back to the field, he was very unhappy. He shot three arrows and told the helper to get them. "The arrows are farther away," he called to the helper.

Then David knew that King Saul was still very sick. David knew he might never be able to live with the King and with Jonathan again.

A little later, Jonathan found a way to talk with David in secret. "My father really is going to try to kill you," said Jonathan. "But I will always be your friend."

"And I will always be your friend, Jonathan," said David.

The two men cried. David and Jonathan knew they might never see each other again. They gave each other a hug.

Then David went away to hide in the hills. And Jonathan walked slowly back to the palace.

David and Bathsheba

2 Samuel, 11 & 12

When David grew up, he became a very famous leader of the people of Israel. David fought in many wars and many people thought he should be the King. But David said, "No. Saul is the King."

In one of the wars that the Hebrews were fighting, King Saul and his son Jonathan were killed. David was sorry that King Saul was dead. And he was very sad about his friend Jonathan. David cried for a long time.

After King Saul had died, many of the people wanted David to be King. And David became a very good and famous king.

David built some beautiful buildings in Jerusalem. He made Israel a strong country. David took his army to fight many wars and won most of them.

The most important thing David did was to keep the Hebrew people from fighting with each other. For the first time in many years, the people of Israel got along.

When David got older, he decided one day to stay home from the war. He wasn't strong enough to fight any more. David didn't like getting older and not being strong any more.

Standing high on the roof of his palace one day, David looked down at the other houses. He saw a woman named Bathsheba having a bath on the roof of her house. "That lady is very beautiful," thought King David.

Since David was the King, he felt he could take anything he wanted. So he sent one of his servants to tell Bathsheba to come to the palace.

King David made Bathsheba have sex with him, and she became pregnant. Then David decided that he wanted to marry Bathsheba, but she already had a husband.

Her husband's name was Uriah. He was away with the army fighting in the war. So King David sent a message to the general who was leading the army for King David. "Send Uriah to the place where the fighting is the hardest. I want him killed."

Bathsheba didn't like what David was doing. But she had no choice. "I am just a woman," thought Bathsheba. "David is the King." Several months later, Bathsheba gave birth to a baby boy.

There was a man named Nathan who often helped King David decide things. Nathan was a prophet like Samuel. He helped people understand how to live in God's way.

Nathan went to King David and said, "I need your help in deciding something. Will you help me?"

"Of course," said King David.

Then Nathan told David this story.

"Two men live near each other. One of them is very rich and the other is very poor.

"The poor man and his family have no money and hardly anything else. But the poor man's family does own one small sheep. His children play with it, and they even take it to bed with them at night.

"One day the rich man wanted to have a big dinner. A friend had come to visit him. The rich man had lots of sheep of his own. Still the rich man took the sheep that belonged to the poor man. He killed the sheep and cooked it for dinner."

King David was angry when he heard Nathan's story. "That rich man was bad. He should be killed."

"You are that man!" said Nathan. "This is what God is saying to you, King David. 'I made you a great king. You have all kinds of good things. You are very rich. Why did you steal Bathsheba, and then kill her husband?"

Then King David knew he had done a very wrong thing. "I have sinned against God," said King David.

"Yes, you have sinned," said Nathan. "Because of that sin, the child that was born to Bathsheba is going to die."

David was very sorry for what he had done. David loved the child that he'd had with Bathsheba. David prayed very hard to God that the child wouldn't die. But the child still died.

And King David learned that even great Kings should live in God's way. He had other children, but he never forgot the one who died.

A Very Wise King

1 Kings 3:16-28, 4:29-34

When King David was very old, his sons started fighting each other. They all wanted to be King when David died.

Finally, David said, "Solomon will be King when I die."

Solomon knew it would be very hard to be the King of Israel. He was still quite young, and he didn't really know how to be a King.

One day, God said to Solomon, "Ask for anything you want, and I'll give it to you." So Solomon said, "Please God. Help me to be wise. Help me to know what things I should do and say."

God was very pleased that Solomon had said, "Help me to be wise." God was glad that Solomon didn't ask to be strong or rich. So God said to Solomon, "I will help you be wise. And because you didn't ask for it, I will also make you strong and rich."

Soon Solomon became famous because he was so wise. He always knew what to do with a hard problem.

One day, two women came to him. They lived together in the same house. And they brought a small baby with them.

"This is my baby," said the first woman.

"It's mine!" said the other.

"Wait a bit," said King Solomon. "Tell me what happened."

"Both of us had brand new babies," said the first woman. "But the other woman's baby died. Then she took my baby and said it was hers."

"I did not," said the second woman. "This is my baby."

"Well," said King Solomon. "I'll take my sword and I'll cut

the baby in two. Then you can each have half a baby."

"Sure. Why not?" said the second woman.

"No! No!" screamed the first woman. "Give the baby to her. Don't cut it in half. Please!"

"Now I know who the baby really belongs to," said King Solomon. He picked up the baby and handed it gently to the first woman. She was the one who said, "Give the baby to her."

"I can tell that you are the real mother," said the King, "because you showed that you loved this baby."

King Solomon did many other things that made him famous. He wrote many songs. He taught people about plants and trees and animals and birds. People from all over the world came to hear what King Solomon had to teach.

Solomon also built a very big temple where people could come and worship God. It was very beautiful and people came from everywhere to see it.

The Prophet Elijah

1 Kings 17:7-24

After King Solomon died, there were many kings. The worst one was King Ahab. He didn't care at all about living in God's way. King Ahab killed many of God's prophets. King Ahab's wife, Jezebel, told people to worship other gods.

Then Elijah the prophet went to Ahab and said, "I have a message for you from God. Because you are worshiping other gods, there will be no rain in Israel for a long time."

That made King Ahab very angry. He wanted to kill Elijah. So Elijah ran far away.

At first, Elijah didn't know where he would stay or how he would get food. But God told Elijah that he would be looked after by a kind woman.

Then Elijah saw a woman gathering sticks of wood for her fire. "Would you get me a little drink of water?" he said to the woman. As she was going to get the water Elijah said, "And could I have a small piece of bread too?"

"I'm sorry," said the woman. "I don't have any bread. I'm gathering a few sticks to take home to make the last meal for my son and me. I have just a handful of flour and a little bit of cooking oil. When we have eaten that, we will starve."

"Don't be afraid," said Elijah. "Go home, and first make a small piece of bread for me. Then make some bread for yourself. There will be enough flour and oil."

The woman did that and found there was flour and oil left over. The next day, she made some more bread, and there was still flour and oil left over.

This went on, day after day. The flour and the oil didn't seem to run out.

Elijah had been staying with the woman for quite a while, yet there always seemed to be enough bread to eat.

One day, the woman's son got sick. Each day, the boy got sicker and sicker, and then he stopped breathing.

"You are God's prophet," she cried to Elijah. "Did you come here to kill my child because of the bad things I have done?"

"Give me your child," Elijah said. He took the boy in his arms and carried him upstairs to his own bed. Elijah called out to God, "Did you do this, God? This woman has been very kind to me. Why did you make this happen?"

Elijah held the boy very tightly in his arms and called to God over and over. "Please let this boy's life return to him."

After a while, the boy began to breathe again. He was alive. Elijah picked him up and carried the boy downstairs to his mother.

"Look," said Elijah, "Your son is alive!"

The woman was very happy. "Now I know that your God is the real God. I know that you are God's prophet."

God Speaks in a Whisper

1 Kings 19:11-13

King Ahab was still trying to kill God's prophets. Jezebel, King Ahab's wife, sent some of her servants to find Elijah and kill him. Elijah was afraid.

"Oh, God," said Elijah. "Everything is going wrong. The people of Israel are turning away from you. They are helping King Ahab and Jezebel kill your prophets. I am the only prophet left. Why don't you just kill me too?"

So God said to Elijah, "Go up to the top of the mountain, and I will speak to you there."

So Elijah went up the mountain. He listened for God's voice.

Elijah heard a strong wind that even blew the rocks around.

But the voice of God was not in the wind.

Elijah felt a mighty earthquake.

But the voice of God was not in the earthquake.

Elijah heard the crackling of a huge fire.

But the voice of God was not in the fire.

Elijah heard a soft, quiet whisper.

God spoke to Elijah in a whisper.

When Elijah heard God's voice, he felt strong enough to keep on being a prophet.

Miriam Smiles

based on 2 Kings 5:1-15

It was the middle of the night. Miriam lay on her mat, listening to Ghazal cry in the next room.

"Miriam!" Ghazal called.

"Yes, ma'am?" said Miriam as she came and stood beside Ghazal's chair. But Miriam already knew what Ghazal wanted because this had happened every night for a long time.

"Rub my neck and my back, Miriam. Help me relax. I've got to get some sleep." Miriam's strong, young fingers rubbed the tight muscles in Ghazal's neck and back. Slowly Ghazal began to relax, and after awhile she fell asleep. Miriam went back to her mat, but she didn't go to sleep.

Miriam lay on her mat and tried hard to remember. Remembering helped when she was feeling lonely. Miriam felt lonely most of the time because she was just a tiny girl, almost just a baby when the soldiers came and took her from her home in Israel. Naaman, Ghazal's husband, had bought her at a slave market.

"Here," Naaman said to Ghazal, "this girl from Israel will be your helper. She will do everything you tell her." And so Miriam worked all the time, even though she was only ten years old. She never went to school. She never had time to play. Whatever Ghazal wanted, Miriam had to do.

But Ghazal was kind, and she liked Miriam. Sometimes she talked to Miriam almost as if she were a younger sister. So Miriam was not unhappy, but oh, how she missed her family and her friends back in Israel. It was so hard to remember them. Each night, before she slept, Miriam asked God to help her remember. God helped Miriam feel strong and not quite so lonely. But still, Miriam felt sad all the time. And she almost never smiled.

The next night, Ghazal called again. And again Miriam

gently rubbed her neck and back. "Do you know why I am so unhappy, Miriam?" Ghazal asked.

"Is it because your husband is ill?"

"Yes. Yes, and not just ill. Naaman has leprosy. It is such a horrible disease, Miriam. So horrible. When his disease gets worse, they will send him away to live by himself, and he will die."

"I can remember a prophet who lived near my home," said Miriam. "They said he could cure leprosy because he serves our God."

"Really? Tell me about the prophet, Miriam. Tell me everything you can remember."

Miriam tried hard to remember. It had been long ago when she was taken from her home. But she could remember the prophet's name. Elisha. And where he lived. Samaria. "But ma'am," said Miriam. "Your husband would never believe the word of a Hebrew slave girl."

"That's true," said Ghazal. "But he must. He must!" Ghazal stood up suddenly, and walked toward her husband's room.

It was a long time before Ghazal told Miriam what happened. Miriam knew that Naaman had gone away for awhile, but nobody told her why.

Then one day Ghazal called Miriam. "Thank you so much, Miriam," she said as she hugged the slave girl. "Naaman is back. He went to your country and he went to see your prophet, Elisha. Naaman hated it when Elisha told him to bathe in the Jordan river. 'We have far better rivers where I live!' he said. But he bathed in the Jordan anyway, and now his leprosy is all cured. He's not sick anymore."

"I didn't think he would believe me," said Miriam.

"Oh he didn't want to, Miriam. I had to argue very hard," said Ghazal. "I told him you talked to your God, and that your God helped you to be strong and to remember the prophet Elisha. God helped you do a wonderful thing, Miriam."

There were tears in Miriam's eyes, but her face showed a big, bright smile.

After the time of King Solomon, there were many wars. And often the Hebrews went to live in other countries to get away from the fighting. Sometimes they had to go to another country because soldiers would take them away.

That is how it came to be that many Hebrews were living in a country called Persia. By this time, many of the Hebrews were calling themselves Jews.

Some of the stories about the Jews in Persia are in the book of Esther.

One of the stories is about a very brave woman named Vashti. Her story helps us understand that God loves everybody. And God wants us to love each other. This means that men are not the boss over women and women are not the boss over men.

Another story is about Queen Esther. God helped Esther save her people from a very wicked person.

The Queen Says "No"

Esther 1

King Xerxes was king of a country called Persia. Xerxes thought he was a wonderful king. King Xerxes thought he was just the most wonderful man in the whole world.

One day he said, "I want to show everybody what a great king I am." So the King brought out all the beautiful things he owned. He brought out all his expensive jewels. He opened up his big buildings. Then King Xerxes said to the people of Persia, "Come! See all my things. See what a great king I am."

Then the King had a party. It was a very big party that lasted for seven days. There was lots of food and wine. Everybody ate and drank too much.

When people drink too much wine, their minds don't work very well. This happened to King Xerxes.

The King was married to Queen Vashti. Queen Vashti didn't always like the way the King treated her. Sometimes the King acted as if Queen Vashti was just a pretty toy that he could show to his friends.

On the seventh day of the King's party, the King said to Queen Vashti, "Come over to the party, woman. I want to show you off to my friends. You can dance for them. Show them how sexy you are."

Queen Vashti was very brave. "No!" she said to the King. "I'm not going to your party. That's final."

The King was surprised. He didn't know what to say. Queen Vashti had never said "no" before.

So the King talked to his friends. "What will I do?" he said.

"This is bad," said the King's friends. "Women should do just what their men say. Men are the boss. If other women hear what Queen Vashti has done, they won't let the men be the boss all the time."

Then one of the King's friends said, "Listen, King Xerxes. You have to show all the women that men really are the bosses. You tell Vashti that she can't be the Queen any more."

That's what the King did.

It was very hard for Vashti to say "no" to the King. When she was the Queen, Vashti had good food, nice clothes, and a nice palace to live in.

Because Vashti said "no," all those things were taken away from her.

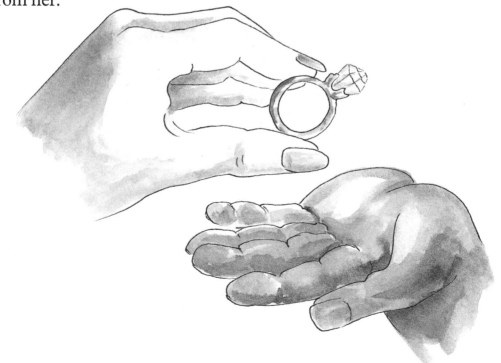

Esther Saves Her People

Esther 2

King Xerxes had said to Vashti, "You can't be the Queen any more."

Then the King's friends said, "Why don't you send your servants all over Persia. Tell them to find the most beautiful girl to come and be the Queen instead of Vashti?"

The King thought that was a fine idea. His servants brought beautiful girls from everywhere for the King to see. He picked Esther. She became the Queen in place of Vashti.

Esther's mother and father had both died when she was tiny. She lived with her uncle. His name was Mordecai.

Esther and Mordecai were Jews. They had come to Persia from Canaan. Some of the people of Persia didn't like the Jews.

One of the people who didn't like the Jews was Haman. He was one of King Xerxes' best friends. Most of all, Haman didn't like Mordecai.

Haman wanted everyone to bow down when they saw him. Haman wanted everyone to treat him as if he were the most wonderful man in the world. Haman wanted to be like his friend King Xerxes.

Mordecai treated Haman just like everybody else. "God made me," said Mordecai. "God made Haman. God made all of us. We're all the same. So why should I bow down to Haman or anybody else?"

That made Haman very, very angry.

One day, Haman said to the King. "There are some people

in Persia who don't obey all your laws. They worship their own God and they are different than other people in Persia."

"What should we do about that, Haman?" said the King.

"Why don't you just let me kill them?" said Haman.

"Fine, fine," said the King. "Whatever you wish."

So Haman told everybody that all the Jews in Persia would be killed. Of course, when the Jewish people heard about this, they were very, very afraid.

Mordecai was afraid too. He decided to do something. He sent a message to his niece, Queen Esther.

"Esther," wrote Mordecai. "Please help us. Try to talk to the King. Tell him to stop Haman from killing all the Jewish people. You are the only one who can help us!"

"The King won't listen to me," thought Esther. "I'm just a woman. I know what the King did to Vashti. He could do the same thing to me."

Esther thought for a long time. Finally she sent a note back to her Uncle Mordecai. "I might be killed," she wrote, "but I will talk to him."

King Xerxes was not a kind person, but he liked Queen Esther. So Esther made him a very nice dinner to make him feel good.

"Did you like the dinner?" she asked the King.

"Oh, yes, it was wonderful," he said.

"Tomorrow night I'll make you an even nicer dinner," said Esther.

That night, the King couldn't sleep. Maybe Esther put too much spice in the food. So the King decided to read a book. It was a book about all the people who had helped the King.

In the book the King read about how Mordecai had once stopped some people who wanted to hurt the King. "I wonder," said the King. "Did I ever thank Mordecai for being so kind to me?"

The King didn't know that Mordecai was Esther's uncle. The King didn't know that Esther was Jewish. The King didn't know it was the Jews that Haman wanted to kill.

That night, the King sat down to dinner with Esther. Esther was very clever. She had invited Haman too. Esther was ready to try and save her people, the Jews.

When they all had eaten a nice meal, Esther spoke to King Xerxes. "Do you remember Mordecai who stopped some people from hurting you?"

"Oh yes," said the King. "I was reading about him last night. He's a fine, brave person."

"Mordecai is my uncle," said Esther.

"We need more people in Persia like you and your uncle Mordecai," said the King.

Esther's heart was beating so fast. She was afraid now. King Xerxes might get angry at what she was going to say. If he got angry, he would kill her.

"Mordecai and I are Jewish," said Esther. "We are some of the people Haman wants to kill. Please, King Xerxes, don't let Haman kill all the Jews!"

Then King Xerxes was very angry at Haman. "You wanted to kill all those people? Well, you shall be killed yourself!"

Esther told Mordecai all that had happened. "Thank you Esther," said Mordecai. "The Jewish people will always remember how brave you were. You risked your life to save your people."

From that time till now, Jewish people remember the story of Esther. Every year Jewish people have a special celebration. It is called Purim. They remember how God helped brave Esther save her people.

Some things are very hard to understand. In Bible times, people wondered – if God wants us to be good people, why doesn't God make it so good people get all the good things?

One way to understand things is to tell a story. Many years ago, somebody made up a story so they could understand why bad things happen to good people.

The story of Job doesn't really answer the question. But it helps us to know that God understands, even when we don't.

The Story of Job

There was a man named Job who always tried very hard to live in God's way. Job wanted to do all the right things.

Job was very rich. He had a nice family, lots of servants and plenty of money. Every day, Job would say prayers to God, and would try to do everything just the way God wanted.

One day, up in heaven, God and Satan were talking to each other.

God said to Satan. "Have you noticed Job? Have you noticed how he does everything just the way I want him to do it?"

"He only does all those good things because he's rich," said Satan. "Take away all his money and his servants. Job won't be such a good person any more. Job will be very angry at you."

"That's not true," said God. "Take away everything he owns. See what happens."

So Satan took away everything that Job had. Satan took away his money, all his children, all his sheep, everything. But Job just kept praying to God and trying to live in God's way.

"See," said God to Satan. "Job is still a good person."

"But if you take away his health," said Satan, "he won't worship you any more. He won't be a good person if you make him sick."

"That's not true," said God. "Go ahead. Make him sick and see what happens. But don't let him die."

So Satan made Job very sick. Satan gave Job sores all over his body. Job felt just awful.

Then three of Job's friends came to him. They felt bad

because Job was having such trouble. "If we visit him," they thought, "maybe he'll feel better."

At first Job's friends just sat around. They didn't know what to say. After a while, they began to talk to Job.

"All these bad things have happened to you because you have done bad things," said Job's friends. "You have not lived in God's way. That's why God is hurting you."

"No," yelled Job. "That's not true. I have tried hard to live in God's way. That's not the reason these things are happening to me."

"It is so," said Job's friends.

"It is not," Job said.

That's when God decided it was time to say something.

"Listen, Job," said God. "You and your friends don't know what you are talking about. Why are you trying to understand this? Where were you when I created the world? Where were you when I made the oceans and the forests and the birds and the sky? What makes you think you can understand these things?"

Then Job knew that he was trying to understand things that were too hard for him. Job said to God, "I know you are very strong. You can do anything you want to do. I'm sorry I was talking about things I couldn't understand. I won't do that any more.

"Up until now, I had only heard people talk about you. Now I have met you and heard you speak to me. I'm sorry for the wrong things I said."

Then God gave back to Job all the things that had been taken from him. Job was healthy again. He even had more children...seven sons and three daughters.

When Job was ready to die, he did something different. In Bible times, most fathers gave their home and farm and money to the boys. The girls didn't get anything.

But Job gave things to both the girls and the boys.

When we go to church, we sometimes sing songs about God. We read the words out of a songbook.

The Bible has a songbook right in the middle of it. It is called "Psalms," and this songbook is full of songs about God.

Some people say the psalms were written by King David. But nobody knows for sure who wrote them.

Perhaps this first psalm was written by a shepherd. Maybe the shepherd thought God must be like a good shepherd who really wants to take good care of the sheep.

Songs from the Bible

Psalms 22, 23 & 150

Psalm 23
I think of God as my shepherd
Who gives me all that I need;
Who lets me lie down,
On soft green grass,
Beside a quiet stream.

I think of God as my shepherd,
Who helps me do what is right.
God helps me feel strong
When I'm weak and afraid;
When I'm crying
For someone who's sad.

My shepherd is glad when I'm happy,
And gives me good things to eat.
I know I'm invited
To live in God's house
For all the days of my life.

Some of the psalms were written by people when they were feeling hurt, or angry, or lonesome or afraid. Here is a psalm that Jesus remembered when he was hurting.

Psalm 22 (selected verses)
My God, my God,
Why have you gone away from me?
Why are you so far away –
So far you can't hear me crying?

Right now I feel like a worm,
And my friends are mean to me.
People make fun of me.
They say bad things and make faces at me
Because they know I believe in you.

Oh God, you helped me when I was born.
I learned to trust you
When my mother was feeding me milk from her breast.
As soon as I came out of my mother's body
And she held me in her arms
I learned to trust you.
Please God,
Don't be far away from me
Now when I am in trouble.

I know I can count on you, God,
Because you have always helped people
When they were hurting,
When others were angry at them,
When they were afraid.

So I will keep telling others about you, God,
Because even though you feel far away,
I know you are here with me.
Always.

Some psalms were written when people felt very happy.

Psalm 150
Make happy
sounds for God!
Make happy sounds
for God in church.
Make happy sounds for God
Who is everywhere.
Make happy sounds for God
Who has done great things.

Make happy sounds with a trumpet.
Make happy sounds with a harp.
Make happy sounds with drums and bells,
Make happy movements with your body.
Dance for God!

Make happy sounds for God
With fiddles and flutes.
Make happy sounds for God
With loud crashing cymbals.

Let everything that can move and breathe,
Make happy sounds for God!

Song of Songs is a book of love songs. They are the words to songs which were sung long ago when a woman and a man were in love.

Song of Songs

(selected verses)

Woman:
Kiss me again and again,
For your love is sweeter than wine.
I will be happy whenever you are with me.

Man:
How beautiful you are, my darling!
How very beautiful.
Your eyes remind me of doves.

Woman:
I am like a beautiful flower,
Like a lily that grows in the valley.

Man:
Like a lily among thorns,
My love is more beautiful than anyone else.

Woman:
How handsome you are, my lover,
Like a deer that runs in the mountains.
Come my love,
The time of the rains is over and gone,
The time of singing of birds has come,
And the voice of the dove
Is heard in the land.

Man:
How beautiful you are, my darling.
Your lips are like a red ribbon,
Your breasts are like two young deer.
You are beautiful, my darling.

Woman:
My lover is tanned and handsome,
His hair is curly and black.
His cheeks are like sweet flowers,
And his lips are like lilies.
His body is strong.
His legs are like two strong posts.

Man:
How beautiful you are, like a princess.

Woman:
Come with me, my lover,
And run with me,
Like a deer runs in the mountains.

Isaiah was in the temple which King Solomon had built. Isaiah had gone to the temple to pray to God. While he was in the temple, something wonderful happened to Isaiah. This is how Isaiah told the story in the Bible.

The Story of Isaiah

Isaiah 1 – 39

I had my eyes closed while I was praying to God. But even with my eyes closed I could see something happening.

I could see God sitting on a big chair with angels all around. I could even hear what the angels were saying.

"God is wonderful," said the angels. "Everything in the whole world shows us God's beauty."

Then I remembered that I hadn't always lived in God's way. Sometimes I said things that weren't true.

"What is going to happen to me?" I cried. "I have said things I shouldn't have said. So have my friends and family. Oh God, what are you going to do to me?"

With my eyes still closed, I could see one of the angels take a red hot coal. The angel came and touched it to my lips.

The angel said to me, "See? This hot coal has touched your lips. God knows you are sorry for the things you have done."

Then I heard God's voice. "I need someone who will talk to all my people about me. Who can I send?"

All of a sudden I heard my own lips saying, "Here I am. Send me."

When I opened my eyes I was still there in the temple. There were other people in the temple, but they acted as if they hadn't seen or heard anything.

I knew then that God wanted me to be a prophet. God wanted me to go and tell the people. God wanted them to hear and understand too.

Isaiah's Message

A prophet teaches people how to grow and live in God's way.
Here are some of the things Isaiah said.

Stop doing wrong things.
Learn to do right things.
Try to be fair to other people.
Help those who are sad or who are hurting.
Help people who don't have anyone to look after them.

Even though you have done very bad things,
If you are sorry, God won't be angry any more.

Sometimes Isaiah talked about a special leader who would show the Hebrew people how to love God.

A child will be born for us,
A child who can show us how to live.
And this is the name for the child:
Wonderful Teacher, Strong God,
A Leader for Peace.

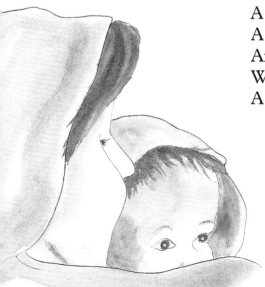

Many years later another prophet said things that reminded people of Isaiah. So they put this prophet's words in the same part of the Bible. They called him Isaiah too.

A Servant Leader

Isaiah 40 – 53

These are the words God sends to you.
There is someone calling:
"In the lonely places,
get ready for God to come.
In the wild and scary places,
make a way for God.
All the dark hollows will be filled up
And all the sharp bumps made smooth.
Then the smile of God will be shown to us,
And everyone will see it together."

This second Isaiah also talked about the leader God would send. When other people talked about this special leader, they hoped for a king or a fighter. But this second Isaiah said the great leader would be more like a servant. This leader would help and care for people.

Do you believe what I have said?
Do you understand what I have said?

The people didn't like my servant.
They thought he was ugly.
They called him stupid.
They laughed at him.

But his bones broke doing *our* work
He got sick so that *we* could stay well,
He got beaten up protecting *us*.

He didn't cry
And he didn't complain.
My servant knew he was doing
what God wanted him to do.
But we thought God
must be punishing him.

This servant hurt
because of *us*.
He was in pain,
because *we* did wrong.
He was punished
for what *we* did.

But,
because he felt the pain
we should have felt,
we are healed!

The Story of Jeremiah

(Jeremiah, selected portions)

Jeremiah was another prophet, like Isaiah. Before Jeremiah was grown up, God came and talked to him.

"Before you were in your mother's body; before you were born, I chose you. I decided you should be a prophet."

"But God," said Jeremiah. "I don't know the right words to say. I'm just a child."

"Don't say you're just a child," said God. "You must tell people the things they need to know about me."

Jeremiah felt as if God had touched his lips. "I will help you know the right words to say," said God.

So Jeremiah started talking to people, telling them about God. Sometimes people got very angry at Jeremiah. They didn't want to hear what God had to say to them.

"Mind your own business," they told Jeremiah. "We can do anything we want. We don't care about God."

One day God asked Jeremiah to go to a place where people make clay pots. Jeremiah watched as a potter tried to make nice round pots.

When the pots didn't turn out right the potter mushed the clay into a lump again.

"Aha," said Jeremiah. "Now I see what God is like."

So Jeremiah went back to the people and said, "You are like clay in God's hands. God has tried very hard to make the

Hebrew people be good people. But if you don't try to live in God's way, God will do just what that potter did."

"What's that?" asked the people.

"God will smash you back into a lump and start all over."

The people just laughed. They didn't care what Jeremiah said. Sometimes that made Jeremiah very angry. Sometimes it made him very sad. But Jeremiah kept trying.

One day Jeremiah got so angry, he went to the potter's house and got a really big pot. Then Jeremiah went back to the people.

"Look!" he yelled. "This is what God will do to you if you don't start paying attention!"

Jeremiah threw the pot down on the ground. It broke into many pieces.

But the people still wouldn't listen.

Jeremiah reminded the people about the promise God had made to Abraham and Sarah and to all the others.

"Remember the promise. Remember the covenant when God said, 'I will be your God and you will be my people.'

"Listen," said Jeremiah. "The time is coming when God will make a new covenant with you. It will be a covenant written down inside you. It will be written on your hearts. Then the people of God will live every day knowing how much God loves them."

A King Learns about God

Daniel 3

A king with a long name brought his soldiers to fight against the Hebrew people. The king's name was Nebuchadnezzar.

The king and his army captured some of the people. He took them back to his own country called Babylon. There he made them work as servants in the palace.

One day the king decided to make a huge statue. Then he gathered all the people together.

"I have some people here to make music," the king said to the people. "Whenever you hear the music, you must bow down and pray to my big statue."

Three of the Hebrew people the king had captured were Shadrach, Meshach and Abednego. They knew the king would be angry if they didn't do what they were told.

"We can't pray to a statue," they said. "A statue can't hear what we say. But our God can hear us when we pray."

When the king heard about this, he was very angry. "Why won't you bow down and pray to my statue?" said King Nebuchadnezzar. "I told everybody to bow down to my statue."

The three friends tried to explain. "We pray to a living God," they said. "We can't bow down and pray to a statue."

The king yelled at Shadrach, Meshach and Abednego. "Just for that, I will make a very hot fire. A big hot fire inside a huge furnace. And I'm going to throw you in there so you will die."

"Tie their hands and feet," the king said to the guards. "Throw them into the fire!"

But the king got a big surprise. When he looked into the furnace, he saw four people walking around inside the fire.

"Why aren't they dead?" asked the king. "Why are there four people in there? It looks as if the fire isn't hurting them at all. And the fourth one looks like an angel."

Then the king went to the furnace and told the three friends to come out.

"I made a mistake," said the king. "Now I know that your God is stronger than my statue. You believed in your God, and your God has saved you."

Many years ago, long before the time of Jesus, the Hebrew people felt very afraid. They were ruled by a very cruel king from another country. The king's name was Antiochus Epiphanes and he hurt the Hebrew people when they tried to live in God's way.

One of the old people, an elder, remembered some stories about a man named Daniel – stories that came from a long time before. To help the Hebrew people not be afraid when the king was being cruel, the elder made up some new stories about Daniel.

Here is one of the stories.

Daniel and the Lions

Based on Daniel 6

Daniel lived in a country called Babylon. He lived there because the king of that country sent his army to Israel to capture a lot of people. "You have to come and live in our country and do our work for us," said the king of Babylon.

Daniel worked hard and soon the king of Babylon said, "Come and help me make the laws and do important things in my kingdom." So Daniel got to live in the king's palace.

Some of the other people who lived in the palace hated Daniel. "The king likes Daniel best," they said, "but we want the king to like us best."

So they made a plan. "Daniel worships the Hebrew God," they said. "He prays three times a day to his God. You can see him pray through the open window." So they

went to the king and said, "Why don't you make a law that says everybody should pray to you. You are the king and so you are a god. Everybody should pray to you and to nobody else."

"Good idea!" said the king.

Daniel knew about the king's new law. But Daniel wanted to live in God's way, so he kept on praying to God three times a day, even though he knew that would make the king angry.

"Daniel doesn't obey your law," said the people who hated Daniel.

That made the king sad. He liked Daniel. "But when I make a law, everyone has to obey. Even Daniel."

So as punishment, the king threw Daniel into a room full of fierce lions. He was sure the lions would eat Daniel. "But I hope your God takes care of you and protects you from the lions," said the king.

The king couldn't sleep that night. He was worried the lions would eat Daniel. The king liked Daniel very much. The next morning he ran to the lion's den. "Daniel, are you all right?" called the king.

"Yes," said Daniel. "My God kept the lions from biting me. They didn't hurt me at all. I love my God very much, and I try hard to live in God's way. God is with me when hard things happen to me."

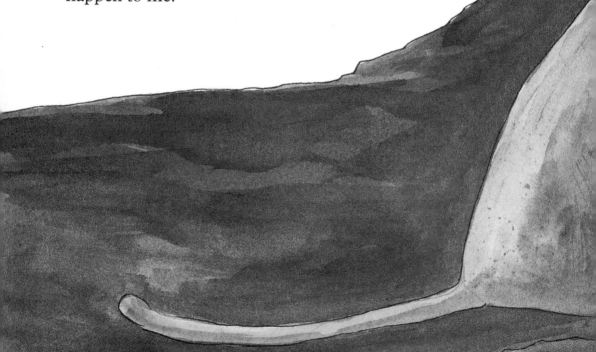

When God's Children Ran Away

Hosea 11:1-11

Hosea was a prophet. Hosea tried very hard to listen to God's voice. Sometimes it seemed to Hosea, that he could hear God's words. Once, Hosea was sure he could hear God crying.

"My children!" God cried. "My children are running away from me. My children, whom I love so much, are running away from home.

"My children, the people of Israel, make me cry. They make me hurt all over. I am their mother. I am their father. I taught them how to walk. I snuggled them up to my face and hugged them. I fed them and took care of them.

"Sometimes they make me so angry. They go away from me and act as if nobody loves them. They fight with each other, they steal, they hate each other, they tell lies. They make me so angry sometimes.

"But what can I do? I love them so much. I get angry but I can't *stay* angry. I can't leave them. I have to go after them and try to show them how much I love them.

"Do you understand that, Hosea?"

"Oh, yes!" said Hosea. "Do I ever. When my wife Gomer went away from me I was sad. Then I felt angry. But I couldn't stay angry with her. I loved her. I went and told her that, and now she and I are together again."

"And I will keep showing my love to my children," said God. "Even when they run away. I'll just keep loving them and hoping they will come back home."

Amos, the Farmer Prophet

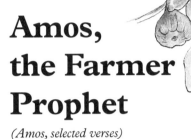

(Amos, selected verses)

Amos didn't really plan
to be a prophet. He knew
how to take care of sheep.
He knew how to grow
nice fruit on fig trees.

It surprised Amos
when God asked him to
be a prophet. "I'm a farmer," Amos said to God. "But if that's
what you want me to do, I'll do it."

So Amos looked around. He saw how the poor people had
hardly anything to eat. They had no place to live. Amos also
saw that rich people lived in very big houses. They ate too
much and got fat. Often they got rich by cheating the
poor people.

Amos noticed that many people were slaves. A slave belongs
to someone else. Like a horse or a dog. If you were a slave, your
owner could hit you or even kill you.

Then Amos knew what God wanted him to say.

"Listen to God," said Amos. "'These people sell other
people for money. The poor slaves get sold for the price of a
pair of shoes. The rich walk all over the poor, the way they walk
on the ground. If you don't stop treating people this way, God
will punish you.'"

Of course, people hardly ever listened to the prophets. They didn't want to hear what God was telling them.

Amos kept trying.

"Listen to God's words," Amos said. "'I hate it when you get together and have a big feast. I can't stand the fancy meetings you have. I hate the songs you sing. They are like noise to me. I won't listen to them.

'This is what I want. I want justice. I want justice when everybody is fair to everyone else. I don't want you to hurt other people or take things away from them. I want you to be kind to everyone.

'I want justice to roll like a river.

'I want your goodness to run

Like a stream that never stops.'"

When people heard that, they talked to their king. "We don't like the things Amos is saying. We want to keep our big houses. We want to keep our slaves. Tell Amos to stop saying those things."

"I'll do even better," said the king. "I'll send Amos back to where he came from. Back to his sheep and his fig trees."

Amos was sad when the king told him to stop being a prophet. He went back to his home. But even in his home, Amos kept trying to help people grow in God's way.

The Funny Story of Jonah

(Jonah, selected verses)

Jonah was just walking along,
minding his business
when God spoke to him.

"Jonah!"

"What?" said Jonah.

"Go to Nineveh and
tell the people that
unless they stop doing
wrong things, I'm going
to destroy them."

Jonah didn't know
what to say. But he knew
he didn't want to go to
Nineveh, whether God
said so or not. So Jonah
ran away. "I'll run away
to Tarshish. That's as
far away as I can get."

Jonah found a boat
that was going to
Tarshish. "Good," said
Jonah. "God won't
find me here on this
boat." So Jonah went
down inside the
boat and fell asleep.

While he was sleeping
a very bad storm came
up. The waves were big.
The wind was blowing.
"Help!" yelled the sailors,
"We're going to drown."

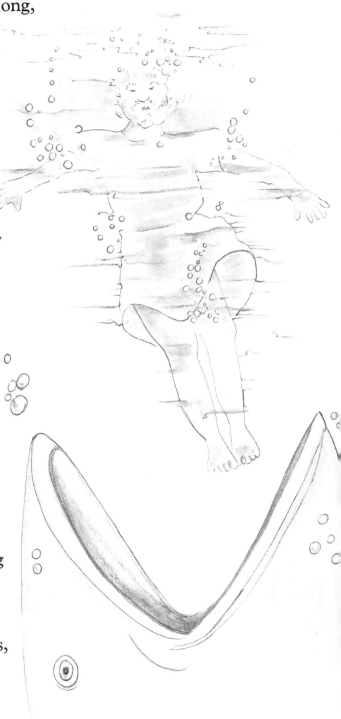

One of the sailors went and woke Jonah up. "How can you sleep when there's such an awful storm? We might drown."

Jonah saw the big waves and the strong wind. He knew what was happening.

"It's all my fault," Jonah said to the sailors. "I made God angry. The only way you can get the storm to stop is to throw me into the water."

"We can't do that," said the sailors.

"You have to," said Jonah. "Or we'll all drown."

So the sailors threw Jonah into the sea.

A great big fish came and swallowed Jonah right up. Gloop!

By this time Jonah knew that when God said "Go to Nineveh," God meant "Go."

"So, all right. I'll go to Nineveh!" Jonah prayed from inside the big fish's belly. "Just get me out of this smelly fish."

Gaaruuuup!

The big fish vomited Jonah out onto the beach.

"Go to Nineveh!" God said to Jonah.

"I'm going, I'm going!" shouted Jonah.

So Jonah went to Nineveh. He went right to the middle of the city and said, "God says to stop doing bad things. If you don't, God will destroy this city."

All the people of Nineveh stopped and listened to Jonah. Even the king said, "He's right, you know. We have not been living in God's way. Let's try to live the way God wants us to, and maybe God won't destroy us."

So God didn't destroy Nineveh. That made Jonah very angry.

"I go to all this trouble and you don't even destroy Nineveh." said Jonah. He sat down just outside of the city. "I'm just going to sit here, God. I might die too. Then you'll be sorry."

So Jonah sat down. The sun came out and it made Jonah feel hot. His stomach felt sick. "I think I'm going to throw up. Maybe I'll die here from the hot sun. Then God will be sorry."

God made a plant come up out of the ground. It grew very quickly. Soon Jonah was sitting in its shade.

"Ah, that's nice," said Jonah. The sun was really hot. "That's a lovely plant."

Then, just as quickly, the plant died. A hot wind came up and the sun was hot again. Now Jonah was really angry at God.

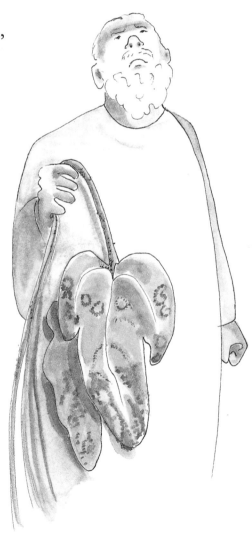

"Why did you kill that plant, God?" yelled Jonah. "I needed the shade. What are you trying to do to me?"

"You liked that plant?" God asked.

"Yes, of course I liked that plant. What do you think?" grumped Jonah.

"So!" said God. "You liked that plant. But you didn't plant it. You didn't help it grow. Don't you think I care about the people of Nineveh? There are many people in Nineveh. And lots of animals. I made them the way I made you. Shouldn't I care about them too?"

The Stories of Jesus

This part of the Bible is called the "Christian Scriptures." Sometimes it is also called the "New Testament."

New Testament means New Covenant, or New Promise. That's because this part of the Bible tells how Jesus showed us a new way to understand God's promise—the same promise God made to Abraham and Sarah many, many years before Jesus.

This part of the Bible is the story of Jesus and his friends. It tells us about the things Jesus said and did. There are stories about when Jesus was a baby and when he was a grown man. And there are sad stories about how Jesus died and happy stories about how he came alive again.

Jesus had many friends. Some of them were called disciples. After Jesus wasn't with them any more, his friends got together and started the Christian church. When they got together as a church, they told stories about Jesus, just as we tell stories about Jesus in our churches today.

Some of his friends wrote the stories down. Other people sometimes wrote letters explaining what Jesus meant. Some of those stories and some of those letters were gathered together and they became part of our Bible.

Now you and I can read those stories and those letters. And when we do, we learn how we can be part of God's plan and how we can live in God's way.

I really like these Christian stories.
I hope you do too.

Ralph Milton

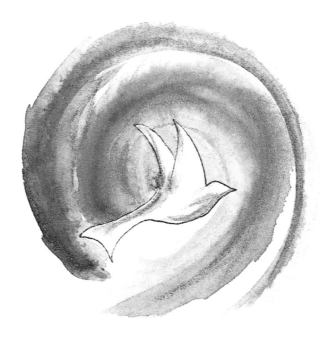

This is the story of how Mary and Joseph learned that Mary was going to have a very special baby.

Mary Learns about Her Baby

Matthew 1:18-25
Luke 1:26-38

Mary and Joseph lived in a small town called Nazareth. They were planning to marry each other.

Late one night, when she was all by herself, Mary felt there was someone with her. She couldn't see anyone. "Are you an angel?" Mary asked in a tiny voice. Mary had never seen an angel, but somehow, she was sure this must be an angel.

Then the someone spoke to her. "Be happy, Mary! God has chosen you for a wonderful thing. You are going to have a very special baby. You must call this baby Jesus, because he will be God's chosen one, God's Messiah."

"But how can that be?" asked Mary. "I'm not married."

"God will make this happen in a way that you will find hard to understand," said the angel.

Mary looked puzzled. "Mary," said the angel, "I will tell you something wonderful that will help you believe me. Remember your cousin Elizabeth?"

"Oh yes," said Mary.

"Elizabeth is growing old. She and her husband were sad because they didn't have any children. But Elizabeth is going to have a baby too."

Mary was glad to hear the good news about her cousin. But she was also afraid for herself. In those days people got angry when women had babies before they were married. She was

afraid people would hurt
her because she was
pregnant. Still, Mary loved
God very much.

"Well," Mary said very
slowly, "If that's what God
wants to do, then that is
what will happen."

When Joseph heard
about this, he was very
worried. "How can Mary
have a baby when we aren't
married yet?" he wondered.

Then one night, Joseph
had a dream. He dreamed
that an angel was telling him,
"Don't worry, Joseph. It's all right.
You and Mary go ahead and get married just as you planned."

So Mary and Joseph
got married, and they
loved each other
very much.

Together, they
planned and worked
to make a loving
home for their
special baby.

Mary Visits Her Cousin Elizabeth

Luke 1:5-25, 39-80

Mary's cousin Elizabeth lived with her husband Zechariah in the hills.

Elizabeth and Zechariah had always wanted to have a baby. But now they were growing old. Sometimes they didn't think they would ever have a child.

One day Zechariah was praying to God in the temple. An angel came, just as an angel came to Mary.

"God will give you and Elizabeth a baby," said the angel. "You will call him John, and he will help many people learn to love God."

Zechariah shook his head.

"You don't believe me?" said the angel to Zechariah. "Then you won't be able to talk until the baby is born."

When Zechariah came out of the temple, he couldn't say a word. He had to write when he wanted to tell people something.

Meanwhile, Mary thought about what the angel had told her. Mary decided that since Elizabeth was also having a special baby, they should get together for a visit.

It was a long walk to Elizabeth's house, but when Mary got near, she forgot about her tired feet. She was so happy to see Elizabeth and Zechariah. From a long way off she called as loudly as she could, "Elizabeth!"

Elizabeth felt her baby move inside her. It was almost as if the baby had heard Mary's call.

"God must really love you," Elizabeth said to Mary. "God especially loves the child who is growing inside of you."

Mary was so happy. She began to sing a song. Some of it went like this:

> How good and wonderful is God,
> How very happy am I.
> God has been so good to me
> that from now on,
> people will remember
> this wonderful thing God has done.
>
> How good and wonderful is God.
> How happy are God's people.
> God has been kind and good to the poor,
> but rich people will get nothing special.
>
> How good and wonderful is God.
> How good and happy are God's people.

Mary and her cousin Elizabeth had a wonderful time talking and laughing. Sometimes they cried a little because having a baby is a little scary. But they could feel their babies growing inside their bodies and that made them happy.

The two women stayed together for about three months. Then Mary decided it was time to go home to Joseph.

After a while, Elizabeth's baby was born. He was a strong, healthy boy. She and Zechariah took the new baby to their church, which was called a synagogue. They wanted to say "thank you" to God, and to give the baby a name. Zechariah still couldn't talk.

Everybody thought they would name the new baby after his father, Zechariah.

"No," said Elizabeth. "The baby's name is John."

All the people in the synagogue looked at Zechariah. They thought he would be upset. Just then, Zechariah found he could talk again. In a loud voice, he said, "His name is John!"

Everyone was surprised. They wondered about the strange things that had happened to Elizabeth and Zechariah while they had their baby. They wondered if the baby would be a special kind of person.

That baby grew up to be called John the Baptist.

Jesus
Is Born

Luke 2:1-7

Mary could feel the baby growing inside her. "It won't be long now," she said to Joseph, her husband.

Then one day Joseph came with some bad news. "We have to go to Bethlehem," he said. "There are orders from the Roman emperor. Everybody has to go to the town that their grandparents came from. The emperor wants to count how many men he can get to fight in his army."

"But the baby is almost ready to be born," Mary said. "It's hard for me to walk very far. Do I have to go too?"

"That's what the emperor ordered," said Joseph. "He wants to count all the people. Because we are part of the family of King David, we have to go to Bethlehem. Bethlehem is King David's city. It doesn't make any sense, but we have to go."

Mary and Joseph were very tired when they reached Bethlehem. They needed to rest for a while, but they couldn't find any place to stay. They tried to get a room in an inn, but all the rooms were taken. Finally, someone said, "You can stay where they keep the cows and donkeys."

It was not a nice place. It was smelly and dirty and cold. But it was the only place Mary and Joseph could find. Joseph felt very angry. "A baby should not be born in a place like this," he said.

That night, in that smelly stable, Mary's baby was born. It hurt when the baby came out of Mary, and she cried. Joseph cried too. He tried his best to help.

Joseph rubbed the new baby dry. Then he wrapped the baby Jesus in some clothes Mary had brought. Joseph and Mary made a soft bed in the straw, and all three of them lay down to rest.

"The angel said this was going to be a very special baby," said Mary. "It doesn't seem very special to be born in a place like this."

"Jesus *is* a very special baby," said Joseph. "But I don't understand either why he should be born here. Maybe someday we'll understand."

Both of them smiled at the tiny, red-faced baby with his eyes so tightly closed. Joseph laughed when the baby closed his tiny hand over Joseph's finger.

Mary and Joseph cried together too. Jesus was so tiny, and the world seemed such a cruel place.

Then Mary and Joseph said "thank you" to God for the gift of their beautiful child.

"Now let's all try to get some sleep," said Mary.

The Shepherds Visit Jesus

Luke 2:8-20

Mary and Joseph and the baby Jesus were sound asleep. They woke up when they heard voices outside.

"Who is it?" called Joseph. The night was very dark. He was afraid someone might want to hurt them.

"It's all right," said a kind voice. "We're shepherds. We've come to see the baby."

"Who told you there was a baby here?" said Joseph. Now he was really worried.

One of the shepherds came inside. "I think it was an angel," said the shepherd. Then all the other shepherds came inside too.

"There was a bright light in the sky," said another shepherd. "And music. Beautiful music."

The shepherds carried bright torches so they could see in the dark. They all stared at the baby Jesus.

"What did the angel say?" Joseph asked.

"First the angel told us not to be afraid," said a shepherd, "But we were scared anyway. None of us had ever seen an angel before. Then the angel told us some good news.

"The angel said a savior had been born, a person who would show us what God is like. And the angel said we could find the baby in a place where they feed cows and donkeys. It doesn't seem like much of a place to have a baby. Especially a baby that's going to be the savior of the whole world."

"It's not a nice place for *any* baby to be born," said Joseph. "What else did the angel say?"

"Nothing," said the shepherd. "Suddenly the whole sky was full of music. There was singing everywhere. The words of the song were something like, 'Glory to God, and peace to all people everywhere.' Then, just as suddenly, the angels were gone."

The shepherds came a little closer. They wanted a good look at Jesus.

"He looks like an ordinary baby to me," said one of the shepherds.

"He *is* an ordinary baby," said Mary. "But he is also special. He is *very* special."

On the way back to their sheep the shepherds told everybody what they had seen and heard.

Jesus Is Presented at the Temple

Luke 2:22-38

After Jesus was born in Bethlehem, Mary and Joseph brought him to the Temple. The Temple was like a big church. It was in the city of Jerusalem. Mary and Joseph had to walk a long way to get from Bethlehem to Jerusalem.

Mary and Joseph went to the Temple to say a special "thank you" to God for their baby. They wanted to promise God to do their best to teach Jesus how to be good and kind to others. "We want Jesus to know about God's promise," they said. "We want Jesus to know that God promised to love everyone."

When Mary and Joseph got to the Temple, a very old man came up to them. His name was Simeon.

God had told Simeon that he wouldn't die until he had seen the Messiah. The Messiah was the one who would show everyone what God is like.

When Simeon saw the baby Jesus, he knew. This baby was God's Messiah!

Simeon was so happy. He took the tiny baby Jesus into his arms and sang a song.

Dear God, now I can die feeling happy.

It was just as you promised.

With my own eyes, I've seen the love

you want to give to everyone in the world.

Then the old man's eyes grew very sad. He looked right at Mary and told her that she would feel great pain sometime because of Jesus.

"It will feel like a sword going right into your heart," said Simeon.

Another person in the Temple was also glad to see Jesus. Her name was Anna. Anna was a prophet. A prophet tells people how to live in God's way.

Anna had lived in the Temple for many years. Now she was 84 years old.

When Anna saw the baby Jesus, her wrinkled face turned all to smiles. And as she walked around the big Temple, she told everyone about Jesus.

Mary and Joseph were tired when they finally got home. But Mary lay awake for a long time, thinking about Anna and Simeon.

There were so many things Mary didn't understand. But she knew that God was with her all the time. When she thought of that, she wasn't afraid any more.

The Magi Visit Jesus

Matthew 2:1-23

After Jesus was born, some Magi came to visit him. Magi are sometimes called The Wise Ones or star watchers.

The Magi were not Jewish like Mary and Joseph and Jesus. They came from a country far away. They said, "We have been looking at the stars. We think the stars tell us a ruler has been born to the Jewish people. Where will we find this child?"

Herod was the king of the Jewish people. He was a very bad person. He was afraid that someone might try to be king instead of him. So when Herod heard what the Magi were looking for, he was afraid.

Herod had a meeting with the people who helped him. "Where do the prophets say that the Messiah, God's chosen one, will be born?" Herod asked.

Herod's helpers looked in all the old books and said, "In Bethlehem. That's what's written in the books."

So Herod talked to the Magi. "This new ruler of the Jews is supposed to be born in Bethlehem. Why don't you go find this child? Then come back and tell me so I can bring him some gifts too."

Herod was lying. Herod wanted to get rid of the baby so it couldn't grow up to be a king.

The Magi went to Bethlehem. They saw a very bright star in the sky. "That star is leading us," they said. "Look! It has stopped moving. That must be the place where we will find the Messiah."

That's how the Magi found Jesus. They gave Jesus some very nice gifts. There was shining gold. There was sweet-smelling incense and a perfume called myrrh.

That night, one of the Magi had a dream. "Don't go back to Herod," the dream said. "Herod wants to kill the new baby."

So the Magi went back to their home by another way.

Joseph also had a dream. In the dream Joseph was told, "Run away. Take Mary and Jesus to Egypt. Herod wants to kill Jesus."

"Wake up, Mary!" said Joseph. "We have to run. We have to run to Egypt!" In the middle of the night, Mary and Joseph and their tiny baby started walking to Egypt. They became refugees – people without a home.

Soon Herod found out that the Magi had not come back to tell him where the Messiah had been born. He was very angry. Herod sent his soldiers to Bethlehem. The soldiers killed all the tiny baby boys in the town. Every one of them.

It was a terrible time for the people of Bethlehem.

The Bible doesn't tell us very much about what happened to Jesus when he was a child. We know that Jesus' family went to live in the town of Nazareth. Joseph was a carpenter. He made things like tables and chairs.

That's about all we know for sure. But we know how other people lived in the time of Jesus. Jesus' life must have been very much like it was for other children.

When Jesus Was a Child

Mary and Joseph taught Jesus how to make things out of wood, how to cook food, and how to be kind to other people. Jesus learned how to tell jokes and sing songs. Jesus liked to play with his friends. He liked to laugh and pretend, just like us.

Jesus liked to hear Mary and Joseph tell the old stories. They told him the stories in the first part of the Bible called the Hebrew Scriptures. (Sometimes the Hebrew Scriptures are called the Old Testament.) These are the stories about Sarah and Abraham, about Isaac and Rebecca, about Miriam and Moses and many other people.

Mary and Joseph also told Jesus about the things the prophets had said and done. They taught him how to sing the songs from the Bible.

Most of all, Mary and Joseph talked about God's promise – about God's covenant. They did things together that helped them remember God's covenant.

Every Friday night when the sun went down, all the people would stop working. This was a special time that Jesus liked best of all. It was the beginning of the Sabbath. The Sabbath began on Friday when it got dark outside. It ended on Saturday when it got dark.

Every Sabbath Jesus' family, just like all the other Jewish people, would wash and put on clean clothes. They lit candles, sang songs, and ate a special dinner. Then they prayed and sang and told more stories.

When Jesus heard the stories and sang the songs, he knew he was part of God's family. Jesus knew that everybody in the whole world is part of God's family.

Jesus in the Temple

Luke 2:41-52

Once a year, Mary and Joseph and Jesus and all the other Jewish people had a very special day. It was called "Passover."

Jesus liked Passover, because he got to do something very important. He was the youngest child. In a Jewish family, the youngest child got to ask a very important question during Passover. While the grownups and the other children sat quietly, Jesus asked, "What makes this night different from all the others?"

The grownups answered by telling stories. They told how God had brought the people of Israel out of Egypt. They told about God's promise to love everyone. God's covenant. They all sang some songs and said special prayers.

And there was lots of food. Special party food. Jesus didn't know which he liked best, the stories or the food.

When Jesus was 12 years old, Mary and Joseph took him to the Temple in Jerusalem. This was a special Passover for Jesus. He was 12 years old. Everyone would treat him like a grownup.

It was called his "bar mitzvah." Jesus was so excited, he could hardly sleep at night.

It was a wonderful Passover. Because Jesus was now a grownup, he was asked to read from the Bible. He read out loud in front of all the other grownups. Then everyone ate and sang and told stories.

The next day, Mary and Joseph started to walk home to Nazareth. Most of their friends and family were with them. There were lots of people all walking together. They had gone quite a long way when Mary noticed that Jesus wasn't with them.

"Maybe he's walking with his friends," said Joseph.

"Well, I'm worried. I need to find him," said Mary.

But she couldn't. Jesus wasn't anywhere with the group of people.

"We'll have to go back to Jerusalem to find him," said Joseph. So they walked all the way back. Mary and Joseph searched all over Jerusalem.

They were tired and cranky by the time they finally found Jesus. He was in the Temple, talking with the teachers. Jesus listened to what the teachers were saying. He asked questions. The teachers listened to what Jesus was saying too. They were surprised how much Jesus knew.

"Jesus," said Mary when she finally saw him. "Why did you treat us this way? We've been looking all over. We were worried sick."

Jesus knew Mary and Joseph didn't understand. "Why were you looking for me?" he asked. "Didn't you know that I had to be in my Father's house?"

Joseph and Mary still didn't understand. "Who did Jesus mean when he said, 'my father'?" Joseph wondered.

Often late at night, Mary thought about her special child. She remembered how he had been born, and what had happened in the Temple.

And Jesus kept growing, like the other teenagers in Nazareth.

Do you remember John? John was just a little bit older than Jesus. John's mother Elizabeth, and Jesus' mother Mary, were cousins. Mary went to visit Elizabeth just before John was born.

John Baptizes Jesus

Matthew 3:1-17
Mark 1:1-11
Luke 3:2-22
John 1:19-36

Some people thought John was weird. He wore clothes made from the hair of camels. He ate insects and wild honey.

Not only that, John often sounded angry. Sometimes he yelled at people.

But John had an important job to do. God wanted John to get people ready for the Messiah, the one who would tell people about God's love.

"Get ready," John shouted. "If you have done wrong things, tell God you are sorry. Live in God's way."

"What do you mean?" people asked John.

"If you have two coats, share with someone who doesn't have any. Be honest. Be kind to others. Don't be greedy."

Many people came to John. "We are sorry for the bad things we've done," they said. "We want to live in God's way."

Then John baptized them in the river. John dipped them under the water for just a moment. Then he lifted them up again.

"I feel washed clean," they said. "I feel clean inside."

"I baptize you with water," John told the people. "But someone is coming who will baptize with something much better. You will be baptized by God's spirit."

One day Jesus came to hear what John was saying. "I want you to baptize me," said Jesus.

"No, no!" said John. "You should baptize me instead."

"John," said Jesus. "God wants *you* to baptize *me*."

John said a prayer, then dipped Jesus under the water and lifted Jesus up again.

Then Jesus and John and all the people around felt God's love in a very special way. Jesus was sure he heard God's voice saying, "This is my child. I love him."

Jesus knew God wanted him to tell people about God. He knew he had to show people how to live in God's way.

But he also knew it would be very hard to do. So Jesus went away to a lonely place to get himself ready.

Jesus Gets Ready

Matthew 4:1-11
Mark 1:12-13
Luke 4:1-13

"How can I show people how to live in God's way?" Jesus wondered.

Jesus went out into the desert. He found a lonely place where he could think for a long time. Jesus didn't eat any food and drank just a little water. Jesus felt that being very hungry and thirsty might help him hear God.

But for a while, Jesus didn't seem to be hearing God at all. Jesus began to hear an evil voice inside him. The voice talked about the wrong way to be the Messiah.

"Look," said the voice inside Jesus. "Here's an easy way to be the Messiah. Turn those stones into bread. If you give people lots to eat, they will say you are the Messiah."

"No," said Jesus. "The scriptures have told us. People need more than bread. They need God's love."

"Well then," said the voice. "Go to the top of the high temple. Jump off. God will help you. You won't hurt yourself. Then everyone will say you are the Messiah."

"No," said Jesus. "The scriptures have told us. Don't try to test God."

"Well then," said the voice. "Go to the top of a mountain. I'll show you all the hills and valleys. I'll show you all the cities and towns. You can be boss of everything if you worship me instead of God. Then everyone will say you are the Messiah."

"No!" said Jesus. "The scriptures have told us. Serve only God. Don't serve anyone else."

"Bah!" said the voice. "I'll get you later."

Jesus was weak from not having any food. He was tired from all the thinking and praying he had done. Jesus knew that being the Messiah would be very hard.

But he felt strong inside. Jesus knew God had been with him there in the desert. God had helped Jesus choose the right way. Now Jesus was ready to show people how to grow in God's way.

Jesus Goes to a Party

John 2:1-11

Jesus and Mary, his mother, went to a party. Some friends were getting married. "Come to our wedding," they said. "We're going to have a really good time."

Jesus and all the others had fun. There was lots of food. They sang and danced.

Then Mary came to Jesus and said, "There's no more wine. Can you help?"

"Why do you ask me?" said Jesus.

Mary was sure Jesus would help their friends. She said to some of the helpers, "Do whatever Jesus tells you to do."

There were six big jars nearby. Jesus said to the helpers, "Fill them with water. Right to the top." So that's what the helpers did.

"Now take some out of the jars and give it to the people," said Jesus.

The helpers did. Everyone was surprised. "This is very good wine!" they said. "Often people serve their best wine first. But this wine is the best of all. It tastes great!"

Most of the people at the wedding party didn't know what Jesus had done.

But Jesus' friends knew. They knew Jesus had come to show people how to live in God's way. Jesus knew that one of the ways to live in God's way is to have fun with your friends.

Nicodemus Comes to See Jesus

John 3:1-21

Nicodemus was an
important man. Late one night, when it was very dark, he came
to see Jesus. Nicodemus had heard stories about things Jesus
had said and done.

Nicodemus wanted his visit to be a secret. He was afraid
people might laugh at him.

"Teacher," Nicodemus said to Jesus. "We know that God
has sent you. Nobody could do all those wonderful things
unless God had sent them."

Jesus looked right at Nicodemus. "Listen to me," he said. "If
you really want to grow in God's way, you must be born again."

"But I'm a grownup," said Nicodemus. "I can't go back
inside my mother's tummy and be born again!"

"That's not what I mean," said Jesus. "You must become a
new person. You must let God's spirit get inside of you. Don't
be surprised when I say you must be born again. When
people are growing in God's way, they feel brand new, like a
tiny baby."

Nicodemus looked puzzled. Sometimes it was hard to
understand what Jesus meant.

"God's spirit is like the wind," said Jesus. "You can't see it.
But you can see the things the wind does. You won't look any

different if you let God's spirit grow inside of you. But you will feel different. And you will care much more about people."

Poor Nicodemus. He tried hard to understand.

"Think of God another way," said Jesus. "Think about God as light. When the light of God shines on things, you can see them in a new way.

"Some people don't like that. They like it better when no one sees the ugly things they do. But if you want to grow in God's way, God's light helps you see. You can clear out the ugly things in your life and bring in things that are clean and bright."

"I get it," said Nicodemus. "When I'm growing in God's way, I'm clean and bright deep down inside. And nobody knows but me."

Jesus smiled. "God knows," he said. "And others will know because you will be a new kind of person."

In the country where Jesus lived, the people were called Jews.

A country nearby was called Samaria. The people who lived there were called Samaritans.

"Those Samaritans are lazy and stupid," some of the Jews said. Often the Jews were mean to the Samaritans.

Many people also thought women were not as good as men. "Women should work hard, have babies and keep quiet," some of the men said. Most of the men wouldn't even talk to a woman. Sometimes they were mean to women.

That's why this story is important. It shows that Jesus doesn't care whether we are boys or girls, whether we are rich or poor. Jesus doesn't care if we are Jews or Samaritans. He doesn't care about the color of our skin. He doesn't care if we are fat or skinny. Jesus loves everybody.

The Woman at the Well

John 4:5-30, 39-42

One day Jesus was walking through the country called Samaria. He was hot and tired, so he sat down to rest by an old well.

Jesus knew about that old well. People called it Jacob's well. Many years ago, the well had been used by Jacob and Rachel and Leah. It reminded Jesus of God's promise to Jacob and Rachel and Leah. God promised to love them and be with them always.

While Jesus was thinking about these things, a Samaritan woman came to the well to get some water. "May I have a drink too?" Jesus asked the woman.

"What? You are a Jew," she said. "I am a woman and a Samaritan. How come you are talking to me?"

Jesus smiled at her. "If you asked me, I could give you a drink of living water."

The woman laughed. "How can you give me 'living water'?" she asked. "You don't even have a cup or anything to get water from the well."

"If you drink from this well," said Jesus, "you will be thirsty again after a while. If you drink the water I give you, you will never be thirsty again."

The woman understood. Jesus was talking about God's spirit. When God's spirit comes into you, it's like a drink of fresh, cool water.

"Please, give me some of this living water," the woman asked Jesus.

Jesus and the woman had a good talk together. They talked about Jews and Samaritans and about the many ways people worship God.

After a while, Jesus' friends came by. They had gone into the town to buy some food.

Jesus' friends were very surprised to see Jesus talking to a woman. Especially a Samaritan woman. But they didn't say anything.

The woman was so excited about her new friend. She ran into her town and told all the people what happened. They invited Jesus to come and stay with them.

Jesus stayed for two days. He talked with the Samaritans about God. Jesus reminded them that God's promise was for Jews, and for Samaritans, and for everyone. Jesus helped them grow in God's way.

Jesus Helps a Child

John 4:46-54

One day a man came running up to Jesus.

"Sir," said the man. "My child is very sick. I'm afraid he is going to die. Please! Please come to my house and help him get better!"

Jesus looked at the man. He could see tears in the man's eyes.

"Go back to your home," said Jesus. "Your child will get well."

So the man walked toward his home. While he was still a long way from home, someone came running out to him. "Your son is feeling better," he was told.

"That's wonderful," said the man. "When did this happen?"

"At one o'clock."

"One o'clock!" said the man. "Why, that's exactly the time I was talking to Jesus."

Simon Gets a New Job

Matthew 4:18-22
Mark 1:16-20
Luke 5:1-11

Simon was tired. He had been trying to catch fish all night long. But there didn't seem to be any fish.

Simon was cleaning his fishing net on the shore. He saw Jesus walking toward him. A crowd of people were following Jesus.

"Simon," called Jesus. "May I use your boat?"

"Sure," said Simon. "Why?"

"If you stop it near the shore, I can sit in your boat and talk to the people."

Jesus sat in Simon's boat. Jesus told the people about God's promise to love everyone. Simon listened too.

When Jesus was finished talking to the people, he asked Simon, "How many fish did you catch?"

"There aren't any fish out there," Simon grumbled.

"Sure there are," laughed Jesus. "Get back into your boat and go where the water is deep. Then try again."

"Wow!" shouted Simon after he started fishing again. "Look at all these fish. My boat is full. Look out! It might sink."

It was hard to row that boat full of fish back to the shore. As he rowed, Simon thought about Jesus. He thought about the things he had just heard Jesus saying.

Then Simon felt sad. "I can't live in God's way," he thought. "I tell lies. I get angry. I'm ugly. I do stupid things. Jesus wouldn't want to be my friend."

Jesus was standing on the shore waiting for Simon.

"Simon," said Jesus, "I'd like to talk to you."

"You shouldn't be talking to me," Simon said to Jesus. "I'm not a good person. I do bad things. And I'm not very smart."

"Simon," said Jesus. "I helped you with your work. Why don't you come and help me with mine?"

"But all I can do is catch fish!"

"Fine," laughed Jesus. "Come, help me catch people."

That's how Simon became one of Jesus' special helpers. Other women and men also became Jesus' special helpers. The Bible calls them "disciples."

There are several women named Mary in the Bible. Jesus' mother was called Mary. Jesus also had two good friends named Mary. One of them was the sister of Martha and Lazarus.

Another Mary came from the town of Magdala. That's why she is sometimes called Mary of Magdala or Mary Magdalene.

Mary was one of many women who were Jesus' special friends – his disciples. Susanna was the name of another. And Joanna. Joanna came from a very rich family that lived in the king's palace. Joanna brought some money so Jesus and his friends could buy food and clothes.

The Bible doesn't tell us very much about the women disciples. So I made up my own story about Mary. Perhaps you could imagine your own story about Susanna or Joanna. Or any of Jesus' friends.

Mary Begins a New Life

Matthew 27:55-56, 61, 28:1
Mark 15:40-41, 47, 16:1,
Luke 8:1-3, 24:10

"This will be a hard thing," Jesus said to Mary. "Do you think you can do it?"

"I have to," said Mary. There were tears in her eyes, but Jesus could see she was ready.

Mary had been born in the town of Magdala. She had grown up there. She knew all the people.

But Mary was not happy. Some of the people of Magdala treated Mary as if she was dirt. That was because she had a sickness that made her feel very sad and lonely.

"I feel as if my body is all full of evil spirits," she told Jesus. "I don't like feeling that way."

"What can you do about it?" Jesus asked.

"I should leave. I should just walk away from this evil." Mary was angry.

"Then why don't you?" Jesus asked. "Why don't you come and be one of my disciples? You can help me with God's work."

"I'm scared. I'm so very afraid."

"Doing something hard is like being born," said Jesus. "It must be very scary for a new baby to be born. The baby has to leave a nice warm place. And the baby doesn't know what it will be like after it is born. But if the baby doesn't get born, it will die."

"And I'm a grown woman," said Mary. "But you think I need to be born into a new life?"

"It helps if you remember how much God loves you," said Jesus.

That night Mary walked away from Magdala. She was sad about leaving the people she knew so well. She was angry at the people who had treated her badly.

Mary felt pretty scared. But she kept saying, "This is like being born. God is giving me another chance."

And it was a new life for Mary. Jesus asked Mary to became one of his disciples. It was hard to be a disciple. Sometimes they slept outside in the cold. Sometimes people got angry at Jesus and the disciples.

But Mary was happy. For the first time in her life, Mary felt good and strong inside.

She went to many places with Jesus and the other disciples, showing people how to live in God's way.

Jesus and Mary had long talks together. Sometimes when Jesus had to do hard things, Mary would help him feel strong.

"Remember," she said. "Doing a very hard thing is like being born. It's scary. You don't know what's going to happen. But if you don't get born, you sort of die inside."

"And I'm a grown man and I need to be born. Is that what you're saying, Mary?"

"It helps if you remember how much God loves you," smiled Mary.

Matthew was a tax collector. He helped the Romans get money from the Jews.

The Romans came from far away with many soldiers. They said to the Jews, "You have to do what we say. And you have to pay us money. If you don't, our soldiers will kill you."

The Romans used Jewish people like Matthew to help them get the money. That's why most of the Jewish people hated Matthew.

Matthew's Surprise

Matthew 9:10-13
Mark 2:13-17
Luke 5:27-32

Matthew had done bad things. He had taken money that didn't belong to him. He told lies.

But Matthew was sorry for the bad things he had done. He wanted to be Jesus' helper. He wanted to grow in God's way.

One day Matthew asked, "Jesus, would you come and have dinner at my house?"

Matthew was surprised when Jesus smiled at him. "I'd like that," Jesus said.

So Matthew asked his other friends to come for dinner too. Many of them were tax collectors like Matthew. He wanted his friends to meet Jesus.

Some important people heard about Matthew's dinner party. "Why does Jesus do this?" they asked. "Why does Jesus make friends with such bad people? He shouldn't talk to people who cheat and tell lies."

Jesus heard what they were saying. "I'm like a doctor," he said. "Only sick people need a doctor. I've come to help people grow in God's way."

"Well!" said the important people. "*We* don't need any help from *you!*"

"Matthew and his friends know they need help," said Jesus sadly. "You important people don't know it. But you need help too. A lot of help!"

Mary and Her Friends Help Jesus

Based on Luke 8:1-3

It was hard work.

Jesus and his friends
were going from one
town to another.
At each place they told people how much God loves them.
They would ask people to try to live in God's way.

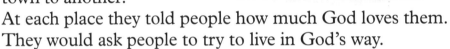

Mary of Magdala was really glad she could go with Jesus
and the other disciples. So were her friends Susanna, Joanna,
and the other women.

It was hard work and it cost a lot of money. Jesus and his
friends needed to have food. He didn't have any money and
neither did most of his friends. But Joanna had quite a bit of
money so she shared it, and everyone was able to get
enough to eat.

Whenever Jesus went into a town, all the sick people would
come and Jesus would try to help them feel better. Peter,
Andrew, Mary, Joanna, and Susanna helped. They would hold
people's hands while they were waiting to see Jesus. And if their
sickness was hurting them and they started to cry, Mary and
her friends would wipe their tears.

If a lot of people came to see Jesus, Mary would ask them to
sit down on the ground, and then she would talk to them about
God's love and how to live in God's way. She would tell them
how Jesus had helped other people.

One night, when Mary was very tired from all the work of

the day, she was sitting beside the lake resting. Jesus came and sat down beside her. "You must be very tired," he said.

"Oh, yes," said Mary. "But when we can help people and tell them about God's love, I feel strong again." Mary sighed. Then she took Jesus' hand. "You must be very tired too, Jesus."

"Yes," said Jesus. "But you help me feel strong too, Mary. You and Joanna and Susanna and Peter and Andrew and all my special friends. When I see you being so kind to people and working so hard, I know this trip couldn't have happened without you. We all had to work together."

Mary looked out at the dark water on the lake. She was still tired, but she felt good inside. She knew she would stay with Jesus no matter what happened, because God was helping her to be strong and kind.

Many people came to Jesus. "Tell us how to grow in God's way,"
they said. Here are some of the things Jesus said to them.

Things Jesus Said

Matthew 5:14-16, 43-47, 6:25-33, 7:12
Luke 6:27-35

When you're growing in
God's way, you are like a
bright light. Others can learn
about God because of you. So
don't hide your light. Let everyone see
what God is like because of the way you are living.

Some people have told you to hate your enemies. They say,
"If someone is bad to you, you should try to hurt them."

I tell you something different.

Love your enemies. Be kind to those who hurt you.

Don't just be nice to your friends. Anyone can do that!
Be good to those who are mean to you.

If someone asks you for help, help them gladly. But when
you help, don't look for praise. Don't say, "Look how wonderful
I am." When you give money to help someone, don't tell
anyone. God will know you did the right thing. And you'll know
you are growing in God's way.

Don't worry about what might happen to you. Don't worry
about what you will eat or what you will wear or where you will
live. God knows you need all these things.

Look at a flower. See how beautiful it is? The flower doesn't
work. The flower doesn't worry. The flower doesn't have any
money. Even King Solomon with all his fine clothes wasn't as
beautiful as a flower.

If God loves a flower, think of how much more God loves you.

So don't worry about what will happen to you. God knows
what you need. God will always be with you.

Finally, here is one thing to remember always. Be kind to
others, just as you'd like them to be kind to you.

Many people came to hear Jesus teach. Sometimes crowds of people came. They followed Jesus wherever he went. Often Jesus sat on the side of a hill. That way people could see him while he talked. Here are some of the things Jesus said about growing in God's way.

Jesus Teaches

Matthew 5:1-10
Luke 6:20-23

If you feel very small inside,
Be happy.
God's love is yours.

If you feel very sad inside,
Be happy.
God will help you feel better.

If you think you are not very smart,
Be happy.
God has a promise for you.

If you try very hard to be good,
Be happy.
God will help you feel good inside.

If you really care about other people,
Be happy.
God cares about you.

If you try hard to work for peace,
Be happy.
God says "You are my child."

If people are mean to you because you love God,
Be happy,
You will always be part of God's family.

The prayer Jesus taught is sometimes called "The Lord's Prayer" or "The Our Father."
You might want to ask someone to teach you the prayer the way it is in your Bible or the way
it is said in your church.

Jesus Teaches Us to Pray

Matthew 6:9-13
Luke 11:1-4

Jesus' special friends,
his disciples, tried hard
to grow in God's way.
They noticed
that Jesus often
prayed to God.
   The disciples
wanted to pray to God,
but sometimes they
didn't know what to say.
One day they asked Jesus.
"Please, teach us to pray."
   "When you pray," said
Jesus, "here are some words you can say:

   Our Father in heaven,
   Your name is holy.
   May your peace come.
   May we live on earth,
   As you live in heaven.
   Give us enough to eat each day.
   Forgive us the bad things we have done,
   As we forgive those who have done bad things to us.
   Don't test us with things too hard for us,
   And save us from evil."

*In Jesus' day, people didn't have cars or airplanes to travel in.
If they wanted to go somewhere, they had to walk. And there
was no pavement so the roads were very dusty.*

> *When people came to visit, their feet felt hot and dusty.
It felt so good to have someone wash their feet. It was a
very kind thing to do.*

The Woman
who
Washed
Jesus' Feet

Luke 7:36-50

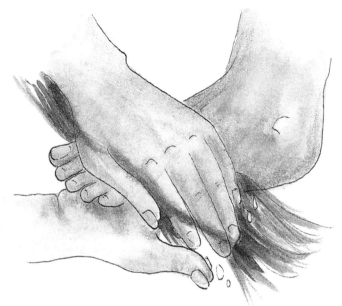

"Will you come to my
house for dinner?" a
man asked Jesus. The
man was a Pharisee, a
very important leader.

There was lots of food on the table at the Pharisee's house.
Jesus could tell that the man had plenty of money. He had lots of
servants. But he didn't bother to have anyone wash
Jesus' feet.

While they were eating a woman came running into the
house. Her dress was torn. She was thin. She
was dirty. Many awful things had happened to
her, and she had done some bad things too.

The woman came up to Jesus. She was
crying. She let her tears fall on Jesus' dusty feet.
Then she kissed his feet and wiped them clean and dry with her
hair. She opened a jar of perfume and rubbed it on Jesus' feet.

When the Pharisee saw this, he frowned. "Doesn't Jesus know
who this woman is?" he thought. "Doesn't he know that she has
done bad things? If Jesus really is a prophet, he'd know she
shouldn't be touching him at all."

Jesus could see the Pharisee's face. He could guess what the man was thinking.

"I have something to say to you," Jesus said.

"Of course, teacher." The Pharisee was very polite.

Jesus told a little story. A parable.

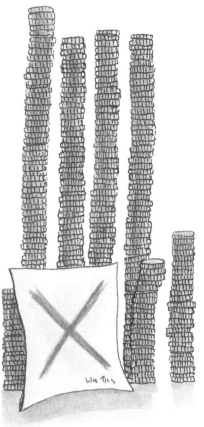

"Two people owed some money to a banker. One owed two hundred dollars. The other owed only two dollars. They didn't have any money to pay it back. So the banker said to each of them, 'You don't have to pay it back.'

"Now," asked Jesus, "which one will love the banker more?"

"The one who owed the most," said the Pharisee.

"That's right," said Jesus. "When I came into your house, you didn't do any nice things for me. You didn't wash my feet. But this woman has washed my feet with her tears. You didn't give me a kiss. But she hasn't stopped kissing my feet.

"Life has been hard for this woman," said Jesus. "So God will reach out to her. She feels God's love more than you do. Those who need more love will be given more love."

Jesus liked stories. He remembered the stories Mary and Joseph told him when he was a child.

Some of the stories were about people like Abraham and Sarah, Rebecca and Isaac, Moses and Miriam.

Sometimes Joseph and Mary made up stories. Made-up stories are fun.

When Mary and Joseph wanted Jesus to understand something, they made up a story. Stories that explain things are called parables. Jesus liked parables.

Jesus made up stories too. Sometimes he made up stories just for fun. Sometimes he made up parables so people would understand about God's love. Those stories helped people grow in God's way.

People liked those parables. "We can understand Jesus because he explains things with stories," they said.

Here are some of the parables Jesus told.

Stories about God's Shalom

Matthew 13:3-12, 18-23, 31-33, 44
Mark 4:3-9, 13-20, 30-32
Luke 8:5-15

The farmer went out to sow some seeds. He wanted to grow some grain to make bread. "I'm going to plant lots of seeds everywhere," said the farmer.

The farmer put a bunch of seeds where people walked. But the ground was too hard. Then birds came and ate the seeds.

"Well, that didn't work," said the farmer.

So the farmer put a bunch of seeds in rocky places. There was hardly any soil. At first the seeds grew very fast. Then they died, because there was no soil for the roots to grow into.

"Well, that didn't work," said the farmer.

So the farmer put seeds among the weeds. The seeds started to grow. But the weeds grew faster and killed the grain seeds.

"Well, that didn't work," said the farmer.

Then the farmer put seeds on good soil. The soil was nice and soft. There was lots of water. Soon the seeds grew into good strong plants.

"Well, that really worked," said the farmer. "Now I'll have lots of grain to eat."

When Jesus told the story, his friends looked very puzzled.

"We don't know what the story means," they said. So Jesus told them.

"God is like that farmer," said Jesus. "God plants lots of love in our hearts. But somebody has hurt us and the love doesn't grow.

"Or sometimes we are very happy when we feel God's love. We sing and dance. But later, we forget about it.

"Or sometimes we're too busy. Or we think about too many other things. We don't have time for God's love.

"Sometimes we let God's love really grow inside us. When that happens, we love other people. Then they know about God's love too."

*Shalom is a Hebrew word. It means something like "peace" but it means more than that.
Jesus told many parables to help us understand Shalom. Maybe he was laughing a little
when he told this one.*

"God's Shalom is like a mustard seed," Jesus said as he held the
tiny seed in his hand. "See how tiny it is?"

"You think a mustard seed can only grow into a small
plant? Well, pretend that it can grow big as a tree. Pretend that
birds will come and make nests in its branches."

Everyone laughed. "A mustard plant as big as a tree?"

"Yes," Jesus laughed too. "God's Shalom is like that."

Then Jesus told an even funnier story.

"You know the yeast people use to make bread? You can't see how the yeast works. It just bubbles around inside the bread.

"Well suppose a woman took a tiny bit of yeast. Suppose she mixed it with a lot of flour and water. The yeast would work inside the dough. After a while she would have enough bread to feed a hundred people!"

"You mean one tiny bit of yeast could make all that flour into bread?" someone asked.

"That's right," Jesus smiled. "God's Shalom is like that. You can't see it working. But it's there, all the time, working in you and working in me."

"Here is another way to think about God's Shalom," said Jesus.

"God's Shalom is like a treasure hidden in a field. If you knew about that treasure, you would go and sell all the things you had. Then you would take the money and buy the whole field. You would want the treasure to be yours."

"Should we want God's Shalom that much?" the people asked.

"Yes," said Jesus. "That much!"

A Child Helps Jesus

Matthew 14:13-21
Mark 6:31-44
Luke 9:10-17
John 6:1-13

Jesus needed a rest.

"Let's go off by ourselves," Jesus said to his special friends, the disciples. "I'm tired. I need to get away from all these people."

So Jesus and his disciples got into a boat. They rowed right across a lake.

But the people followed Jesus anyway. They wanted to hear Jesus tell them how to grow in God's way. A whole crowd of people ran around the edge of lake. Instead of being alone, Jesus and his friends still had a big crowd with them.

Jesus was tired. But he felt sorry for the people. They reminded him of sheep that needed a shepherd to look after them. So Jesus sat down and talked to them about God's love.

"It's getting late," said Philip, one of the disciples. "We should tell the people to go home so they can get something to eat."

"Why don't you give them something to eat, Philip?" Jesus asked.

"There are thousands of people here," said Philip. "We're way out in the country. There's no place to buy food. And we don't have money."

One of the children in the crowd heard Jesus and his friends talking. "I have something we could eat," the boy said to Andrew.

"What have you got?" asked Andrew.

"Five loaves of bread," said the boy. "And two small fish."

Andrew laughed. "Look at all these people! How many could you feed with five loaves of bread and two tiny fish?"

The boy felt sad. He knew it wasn't much but he wanted to share.

"Have the people sit down on the grass," Jesus said. Then he smiled at the boy. "It's very kind of you to share your food. Let's say 'thank you' to God. Then we can eat."

The disciples passed out the food. Everyone ate as much as they wanted. When all the people were full, there was still lots of food left over.

"How did that happen?" the boy asked.

Jesus smiled. "When people are willing to share, there's always enough for everyone. Thank you for showing us how to share."

The Poor Woman's Gift

Based on Mark 12:41-44 & Luke 21:1-4

"Look at me," said the rich man. "See how much money I am giving to God!" The man put a big bag full of gold coins into the box.

Jesus and his friends were watching. They were sitting in the temple, where there were boxes for people to put money into. The money was to pay for things in the temple such as fixing the walls or buying food for the people who worked there. Giving money to the temple was like giving money to the church.

Jesus was glad people gave money to the temple. But Jesus didn't like the way some people bragged about how much they gave.

"I'm giving even more money than that!" said another rich man as he put a bigger bag of money into the box. Jesus shook his head. He was sad.

Then a very poor woman came by – a woman who didn't have any family. All she had was two tiny little coins. When she thought nobody was looking, she went and put them into the money boxes.

"Look," Jesus said to his friends. "She gave the biggest gift of all!"

"But all she put in was two tiny little coins," said his friends.

"It was easy for the rich people, because they still have lots more money at home. It was very hard for the woman to give those two small coins."

"But..."

"When those rich men go home tonight, they will have lots to eat. But the poor woman won't have as much to eat because she gave her money to God. She gave all she had."

The Woman who Touched Jesus

Matthew 9:20-22
Mark 5:24-34
Luke 8:42-48

Often, crowds of people came to Jesus. There were so many people, it was hard to get close to him.

A woman stood on the edge of the crowd. She wanted badly to get closer to Jesus. But she was shy. She was afraid Jesus would be angry if she bothered him.

The woman felt very unhappy. She had been sick for a long time. She had gone to many doctors, but they hadn't made her any better.

"If I could just get a little closer to Jesus," she thought. "Even if I could just touch his clothes, maybe that would help."

The woman pushed through the crowd. People didn't want to move. All of them wanted to be close to Jesus.

"Uhhhh!" She pushed really hard.

Finally she got close enough. Jesus was facing the other way. He couldn't see her.

She reached her hand between two people and just barely touched Jesus' clothes. The woman felt something change inside her. "I'm not sick anymore," she said to herself.

Jesus also knew something had happened.

"Who touched me?" he wanted to know.

"There are many people in this crowd," Jesus' friends said. "Lots of them touched you."

"This was different. Who was it?" Jesus kept asking, until finally the woman came up to him. She was very afraid.

"Please don't be angry with me," she said. "I've been so sick for so long. I needed your help."

"I'm not angry," said Jesus. "I'm happy. You are very brave. You trust God's love. You won't be sick anymore. Go in peace."

Jesus Helps a Sick Girl

Matthew 9:18-19, 23-25
Mark 5:21-24, 35-43
Luke 8:40-42, 49-55

"Please come quick. Please, Jesus," the man cried. "My daughter is very sick. Please come and help her. Please!"

The man's name was Jairus. Jairus was a very important man. He was rich too.

Right now Jairus didn't feel important. Or rich. He felt afraid. "My little girl is dying," he said to Jesus. "Please come to my house to help her."

So Jesus and Jairus hurried toward the house. Before they got there, someone came running. "Don't bother, Jesus. The girl is dead."

Jairus began to cry. Jesus put his arm around Jairus' shoulders. "Don't be afraid, Jairus," said Jesus. "Believe in God's love. And keep walking."

Everyone at the house was in tears.

"Don't cry," said Jesus. "The child isn't dead. She's just sleeping."

Then Jesus took some of his friends and the little girl's mother and father. They went inside. Jesus looked at the little girl. She didn't move. Her face was pale.

"My child," said Jesus. Jesus took the girl's hand. "Get up."

The girl opened her eyes. She looked at Jesus. She looked at her mom and dad. She smiled just a little.

"How old are you?" Jesus asked.

"Twelve," she said.

"Twelve!" said Jesus. "When I was twelve I was always hungry. Are you hungry?"

The girl nodded.

"Good!" said Jesus. "Why don't we see if we can find you something to eat?"

Simon Becomes Peter

Matthew 16:13-26
Mark 8:27-36
Luke 9:18-25

Simon was mixed up. He had been following Jesus for many months. Simon had listened very carefully when Jesus talked. He tried so hard to understand. But often Simon just didn't know what Jesus was talking about.

Simon was one of Jesus' special friends. A disciple.

Jesus often sat with the disciples and talked to them about God. It was like going to school. Or church.

Simon didn't really like this kind of school. "I feel so stupid," he told Jesus one day. "You explain things. Everybody else knows what you mean. But I don't!"

"What don't you understand, Simon?" asked Jesus.

"Well, I've been trying to figure out who you are. Are you a prophet? Are you a teacher? Are you a doctor?"

"Let's see what the others think," said Jesus. Jesus asked all his friends to sit down under an olive tree with him. "Now tell me," said Jesus. "When you are talking to the people who gather around – who do people say I am?"

"Some say you are John the Baptist."

"I heard someone say, 'Jesus is really the prophet Elijah come back to life.'"

"And I've heard people say you are the prophet Jeremiah." Each of the disciples had heard something different.

Jesus was laughing. "Well, I can't be all those people. Who do *you* think I am?"

Simon's face lit up. He had a new idea. "I know. I know. You are the Christ. You are the Messiah. You are the one God is sending to save us all." Simon was very excited.

Jesus was quiet for a long time. He looked at his friends. Then he looked hard at Simon.

"Simon. My friend. God gave you that new idea. You didn't get that idea all by yourself. It's a big idea. It's a hard idea. Your idea is like a big, hard, solid rock.

"So I am going to give you a new name. Your name will not be Simon anymore. It will be Peter. Peter means 'rock'. This idea, Peter, this big rock of an idea, will never go away. All my friends, all the people who follow me in God's way, will remember your idea. Always. It will be like a solid rock they can stand on.

"But for now," said Jesus, "this has to be our secret. The crowds that come to hear me wouldn't understand."

The disciples and Jesus talked for a long time. They had many questions. Would Jesus live in a big palace? Would he have soldiers to fight for him?

"No, no!" said Jesus. "That's not the kind of Messiah God wants me to be. Listen, friends. It is going to be very hard for all of us. The people who have lots of money, the rulers who have big armies, will get angry at me. They will kill me."

"No way!" yelled Peter. "That won't happen to you. No way!"

"Peter!" Jesus sounded angry. "When you talk like that, you are not being my friend."

Poor Peter. Now he was really mixed up. Then Jesus sat down beside Peter. He took Peter's hand.

"It will be very hard for you to be my friends." Jesus spoke very softly. "You won't be rich. You won't be powerful. Many people will hate you. Some people will try to hurt you. Some of you will be killed.

"God's power is the power of love, Peter. That's all. It is very hard to understand. Many people won't like it. It's very hard to live in God's way. Those who live in God's way have only one kind of power. It is the power of love."

Peter was still mixed up. He didn't know how Jesus could be the Christ and still let people hurt him.

But Peter could feel the power of Jesus' love. So Peter felt strong inside. Strong as a rock.

Jesus on the Mountaintop

Matthew 17:1-9
Mark 9:2-8
Luke 9:28-36

"What happened, Peter?" Mark asked.

"I can't tell you. Not now," Peter answered.

"Are you sick? You and James and John. You look so pale!"

"No, we're not sick, Mark." Peter was shaking a little. "Something wonderful happened. But I can't tell you about it. Not now."

Years after Jesus was killed and came back to life, Peter finally told Mark the story.

"Jesus took us to the top of a mountain," said Peter. "It was a long climb. We were tired when we got there."

"Just you and Jesus?" Mark asked.

"No, James and his brother John were there too. They know what happened.

"I'll never forget that time," said Peter. "All of a sudden, Jesus changed. His face shone. It was like looking into the sun. And his clothes turned white. Really white. Then there were two people with Jesus."

"Who?" Mark asked.

"Elijah and Moses."

"How did you know?"

"I don't know how we knew," said Peter. "But we knew. And Jesus was talking to them."

"So what did you do?" said Mark.

"I didn't know what to do. I said to Jesus, 'Shouldn't we build three little houses here? I could build one for you, one for Moses and one for Elijah.' It sounds silly, now that I think about it. But I was so afraid. I didn't know what to say!"

"What did Jesus say?" Mark asked.

"He didn't say anything. A bright cloud came and covered him. Then we heard a voice. James and John heard it too. You can ask them."

"Was it God?"

"It must have been. The voice said, 'This is my Son. I love him. Listen to him.'"

"That's all?" asked Mark.

"That's all!"

"What did you do?"

"We were so scared. We fell flat on our faces. But then we heard Jesus saying very gently, 'Don't be afraid. Get up.'"

Mark was shaking his head. "I don't understand. Every time I think I understand, I hear something new. Then I have to think about it all over again."

"Yeah!" said Peter. "I know what you mean."

Jesus and the Child

Matthew 18:1-5
Mark 9:33-37
Luke 9:46-48

Sometimes the disciples had arguments.

"Jesus likes me better than you."

"He does not!"

"Does so!"

"When Jesus gets to be king, I'll be his favorite."

"You will not!"

"I will so!"

Jesus felt very sad when he heard his friends arguing. "Come over here," Jesus said to the disciples. "I want to show you something."

Jesus went to where some children were playing. One child was sitting alone. "Why aren't you playing with the other children?" Jesus asked.

"They won't let me." said the child.

"Why?" Jesus asked.

"Because my legs hurt. I can't run. I get sick if I run hard."

Jesus picked the child up in his arms. Then he said to the disciples. "Do you see this child?"

"Of course."

"I want you to become like this child. Unless you can be like a little child, you will not be part of God's Shalom."

"I don't get it," said Peter.

"Someday you will, Peter," said Jesus. "But for now, just remember. When you are being kind to a child, you are being kind to me."

Peter blinked. He could see how much Jesus loved the child.

"Here's something else to think about, Peter," said Jesus. "In God's Shalom, the first shall be last and the last shall be first."

Then Jesus looked at the child. "I'd like it if you could play with me. What do you like to play best of all?"

The Lost Sheep

Matthew 18:10-14

"It doesn't make sense, Jesus," Peter said.

"What's wrong, Peter?" Jesus asked.

"You spent two hours playing with that child. You could have been talking to a whole bunch of people. How are people going to know that you are the Messiah? You should be making speeches."

"You can't love a crowd," said Jesus. "You have to love people, one by one. Let me tell you a story about what God is like.

"There was a shepherd. The shepherd had 100 sheep. The shepherd knew each sheep by name. 'Hi, Flop Ears,' the shepherd would say. 'Hi, Spotty! Hi, Mopsy!'

"One night the shepherd was saying good night to the sheep. One of them was missing. 'Where is Flop Ears?' asked the shepherd.

"Right away the shepherd left the 99 sheep safe in their pen. Out into the cold and the darkness the shepherd went. 'Flop Ears, where are you? Flop Ears, it's me! Where are you?' The shepherd called and called and called.

"Then all of a sudden, way down in a deep crack in the

rocks, the shepherd heard 'Baaaaa!' The shepherd knew right away it was Flop Ears. 'I'm coming. Don't be afraid. I'll help you,' the shepherd called.

"They were so glad to see each other. The shepherd hugged Flop Ears. Flop Ears snuggled up to the shepherd. Then the shepherd took Flop Ears back to the other sheep. Everyone was happy again."

Peter understood. "God doesn't want anyone to be lost," he said. "It's hard to think that God cares about one little child. Or about me."

"Yes, it's hard to believe," said Jesus. "But it's true. God loves you. God loves that child."

"What about Flop Ears?" grinned Peter.

"Yes, God loves Flop Ears too!" Jesus laughed.

A Mean Trick on Jesus

John 8:1-11

Some of the Pharisees were angry at Jesus. Pharisees were important people. But people were listening to Jesus. They were not listening to the Pharisees. That made the Pharisees angry.

"Let's trick Jesus," the Pharisees said. "Let's make him say something that is against the law."

So the Pharisees brought a woman to Jesus. "Listen," they

said. "This woman did an awful thing. She had sex with a man who wasn't her husband. The rules say we should kill her. We should throw stones at her till she is dead. What do you think, Jesus? Should we kill her?"

Jesus looked at the woman. She was very afraid. She knew the Pharisees wanted to kill her.

Jesus wondered to himself, "Where is the man she had sex with? Why didn't the Pharisees want to throw stones at him? He broke the rules too."

"You are right," Jesus said to the Pharisees. "She did wrong. So start throwing stones. But someone who has never, ever done anything wrong should throw the first stone."

The Pharisees looked at each other. They knew that nobody was perfect. Each of them knew they had done wrong things. One by one, the Pharisees went away.

Then Jesus spoke gently to the woman. "Where are all the people who said you did wrong?"

"They've all gone," she said.

"Then you can go too. But from now on, try to grow in God's way."

The Good Samaritan

Luke 10:25-37

One day a lawyer came to Jesus. "Teacher," he said to Jesus. "What must I do if I want to live with God after I die?"

"What does it say in the law books?" Jesus asked.

"Love God with all your heart," said the lawyer. "Love God with all your soul. Love God with all your strength. And love your neighbor the way you love yourself."

"That's right," said Jesus. "Do that and you will live with God forever."

The lawyer wanted to argue with Jesus. "But who is my neighbor?" he asked.

So Jesus told him a story about a Samaritan. In the land where Jesus lived, people didn't like Samaritans.

A man was walking down a lonely road all by himself. Suddenly some robbers came. They grabbed the man. They beat him up. The robbers took his money, took his clothes and left him lying on the road. He was bleeding badly.

First came a person who was all dressed up in nice clothes. "Oh," said the well-dressed person. "I don't want to get blood on my nice clothes. I'm going to pretend I didn't see him."

Then a very busy person came along. "Oh," said the busy person. "If I stop, I'll lose some time. I'm very busy. I'm going to pretend I didn't see him."

Then a Samaritan came along. No one expected to get help from a Samaritan. But the Samaritan looked at the man lying beside the road. "Oh," said the Samaritan. "This poor man needs help. I'll see what I can do."

The Samaritan poured medicine on the man's sores. He tore

some of his clothes into strips and made bandages. Then the Samaritan put the man on his donkey and took him to an inn.

"Take care of this poor man," the Samaritan said. "Here is some money to pay for it. I'll come back in a few days. If it costs any more to take care of him, I'll pay you."

When Jesus had finished the story he looked at the lawyer. "Now who was being a neighbor to the man who was robbed?"

"The one who was kind to him," said the lawyer.

"Well," said Jesus. "Go and be like that kind person."

Martha Learns about Food

Luke 10:38-42

Martha liked to help people. She liked to work hard. She liked to make things. Most of all Martha liked to cook. Martha could make wonderful things to eat.

Martha lived in a house with her sister Mary and her brother Lazarus. One of their special friends was Jesus. Martha liked to cook for Jesus. Jesus loved to eat good food.

It was hard work for Jesus to help so many people. Crowds of people followed him everywhere. He talked with them and tried to show them how much God loved them. But it made Jesus very tired.

Sometimes when Jesus was tired, he would go and visit his friends, Martha and Mary.

As Jesus walked toward her house, Martha saw he was tired. "You just go and sit down and relax," Martha said to Jesus. "I'll cook you some really nice food."

Martha thought her sister Mary would help her. Instead, Mary sat down to talk with Jesus. Jesus liked to talk with Mary and Martha.

It was a hot day. Martha was working very hard. She could hear Mary and Jesus talking together in the other room. "Why should I do all this work?" Martha thought. "Mary is just sitting around not doing anything."

Martha was angry. She marched into the other room. "Don't you care?" she asked Jesus. "Don't you care that my sister has left me to do all the work? Tell Mary to help me!"

"Martha, Martha," Jesus said. "Don't worry so much about cooking. You are a very kind person. But you need to sit down and rest a little too. Come and talk with Mary and me."

"Aren't you hungry?" asked Martha.

"Yes, I am," said Jesus. "I'm hungry for your kind of food. I'm also hungry for another kind of food that Mary and I are sharing."

"I don't understand," said Martha.

"There is another kind of food, Martha. It isn't food you eat with your mouth. It is food that helps you grow inside."

Martha wiped her hands and sat down beside Jesus.

"The kind of food you are making feeds us for a day," said Jesus. "But you and I also need God's love. It's a kind of food that feeds us for our whole lives."

"Now I see," said Martha. "We need both kinds of food to be strong."

"That's right," smiled Jesus. "So let's sit and talk for a while. We'll share one kind of food, then after a while, we'll both help you prepare the other kind."

Jesus Talks about Money

Luke 12:13-31

A man came to Jesus and said, "I want you to help me, Jesus. My parents gave some money to my brother and me. But my brother won't give me my share."

"Don't worry so much about money," said Jesus, "Money doesn't make you rich. You are rich when you know that God loves you."

The man shook his head. Jesus could tell he didn't understand.

"Let me tell you a story," said Jesus.

"There was a man who only wanted one thing. Money. He had a big house. He had a big farm, so he grew plenty of grain. He kept trying to get more money. He didn't think about friends. He didn't think about poor people. He didn't think about God. He just thought about money.

"Then one day the man said to himself, 'Finally, I've got enough money. Now I'm going to eat, drink and have fun. I have enough money for the rest of my life.'

"That very night, the man died. He died before he could enjoy his money. He was too busy getting rich to try to live in God's way. He never got to enjoy life."

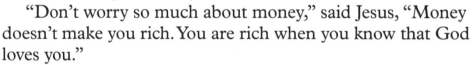

A little later, Jesus was talking to his disciples about this story. Jesus wanted them to understand that it was OK to have money. But we shouldn't worry about it. Other things are far more important.

"Don't worry about what you are going to eat, or drink," Jesus said to his disciples. "Don't worry about where you are going to live. God knows that you need these things.

"Think about the birds and the flowers. They don't have houses to live in. They don't have any money. Still God loves them and takes care of them.

"Don't be afraid, my friends. Give your money away to help poor people. Try to think more about living in God's way. Living in God's way is like having a rich treasure in your heart."

The Bible only tells us a very little bit of the story of the bent-over woman. The Bible doesn't tell us why she was bent over or what Jesus said to her. So I tried to imagine a little more of what happened.

The Bent-over Woman

Luke 13:10-13

One day Jesus was teaching in the synagogue. A synagogue is like a church. It's a place where people come to learn about God.

Jesus saw a woman sitting in the corner all by herself. "Why is she so bent over?" Jesus wondered. "Why doesn't she sit with the other people?

"Maybe people have been mean to her all her life," Jesus wondered. "I think someone has been beating her."

So Jesus called to her. "Would you come over here, please? I have something special to tell you."

Then Jesus spoke to her very quietly so the other people couldn't hear. "I think someone has been very cruel to you. That makes you feel very bad. You feel that nobody loves you."

The woman nodded her head. It was true.

"That person shouldn't be hurting you," said Jesus.

"I just thought it must be my fault," said the woman.

"No," said Jesus. "It's not your fault. It shouldn't be happening."

Jesus was angry. "And it's OK if you feel angry about it."

"I have something very, very important to tell you," said Jesus. "You are God's child, just as I am God's child. You are as important and as good as anyone else. God loves you. I love you."

Then Jesus took her hand and looked deeply into her sad eyes. "Remember, God loves you," Jesus said again. "I love you. You are God's child."

The woman's eyes began to sparkle a little. For the first time in ever so long, she stood up straight and tall.

A Loving Father

Luke 15:1-2, 11-32

Not everyone liked Jesus. Sometimes people got very angry at Jesus for the things he did and said.

"Jesus shouldn't be friends with those people," they said. "We're the important ones. We're the best. Jesus should only be friends with folks like us!"

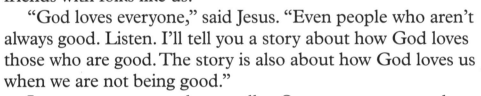

"God loves everyone," said Jesus. "Even people who aren't always good. Listen. I'll tell you a story about how God loves those who are good. The story is also about how God loves us when we are not being good."

Jesus was a very good storyteller. So everyone was ready to listen.

"My story is about a father who had two sons," said Jesus. "The younger son said to his father, 'I hate it around here. If you were dead, then half of your money would be mine.'

"That made the father very sad. But instead of getting angry he said, 'You can have half of my money. Right now. Here it is.'

"So the younger son took the money and left. He went far away from his home. The son spent his money on wild parties and expensive food. He never wrote a letter home. His father wondered if his son had died.

"But soon the money was all gone. The son felt very hungry but now he had no food and no money. So he got a job looking after someone's pigs.

"'This is awful,' he thought. 'Here I am looking after these stinky pigs. I hate pigs. I wish I could go back home.'

"The son knew he had made his father very sad. 'He'd never let me come back home. Except maybe, if I say I'm sorry. Maybe if I just ask to be a helper, a servant, he might let me come home.'

"So the son started walking back home. He was still a long way off when he saw his father running down the road toward him.

"'Father, I'm so sorry....' But his father wouldn't let him finish. His father threw his arms around his son and gave him a kiss.

"Then the father called to everyone. 'Come to our house. We're having a big party tonight. My son has come home! My son has come home! Let's have a party! Let's celebrate!

"They had the biggest party you ever saw. But the father noticed that his older son wasn't there. So the father went looking for him.

"The father found the older son out in the backyard. 'Why aren't you at our party?' the father asked.

"'It's not fair,' said the older brother. 'I stayed at home. I was a good boy. I did all the things you asked. That other son of yours ran away and spent all your money. Then when he came home you had a big party. You never had a party for me!'

"'My son,' said the father, 'I've been able to show my love for you every day. Your brother was lost. Now he's found. I felt as if your brother was dead. Now he's alive. Let's be glad. Your brother is part of the family again!'"

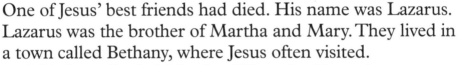

Lazarus Is Alive!

John 11:1-53

One of Jesus' best friends had died. His name was Lazarus. Lazarus was the brother of Martha and Mary. They lived in a town called Bethany, where Jesus often visited.

"Oh, Jesus," cried Martha. "If you had been here, my brother wouldn't have died. You could have helped him."

"Mary. Martha," said Jesus. "Try to believe this. Lazarus will live again."

"We all go to live with God when we die," said Martha.

"That's true, Martha," said Jesus. "We all go to live with God when we die. But that's not what I meant. Show me where you buried Lazarus."

So Martha and Mary took Jesus to the grave where they had put Lazarus' dead body. A crowd of people had gathered around.

Jesus cried. His friend was dead.

"Jesus must have loved Lazarus very much," some of the people said.

"Open up the grave," said Jesus. "Take the big stone away from it."

"But he's been dead for four days," said Martha. "His body will smell."

Even so, they took the stone away from the grave.

Jesus prayed. Jesus prayed hard to God. "Please hear me, God," he said.

Then Jesus called with a loud voice, "Lazarus. Come out of the grave!"

"Ooohhh!" everyone gasped. Out of the grave came Lazarus. He had been dead, but now he was alive.

"Give him some clean clothes to put on," said Jesus.

Some of the people in the crowd were not happy to see Lazarus alive again. They were the Pharisees, the rulers.

"Look at that," they said to each other. "Now all the people will do what Jesus tells them. If people follow Jesus, we won't be as important anymore. Maybe we should try to kill Jesus."

Jesus and the Children

Matthew 19:13-15
Mark 10:13-16
Luke 18:15-17

Jesus liked
children. And
children liked
Jesus.

Children
liked Jesus
because he
smiled at them
and laughed
with them.

Sometimes, the
disciples tried to
make the children go
away. "Jesus is much
too busy," they said.
"Jesus has important
things to say to the
grownups. Go away."

Jesus got upset when
the disciples pushed the
children away. "I want to
be with the children," he
said. "Please don't push
them away."

"But why?" asked the disciples. "Grownups are more important."

"No, they are not!" said Jesus. "Children are just as important. And grownups can learn many things from children."

"But grownups know more than children," the disciples said.

"Grownups know many things," said Jesus. "But they don't *understand* some things. Some children understand loving and trusting better than grownups."

Then Jesus spoke to all the grownups. "I've talked to you many times about God's Shalom. God's Shalom happens when people love and care for each other. Watch the children. Learn from them. Then you will understand God's Shalom."

Jesus could see the grownups didn't know what he was talking about. So Jesus picked up a tiny child, a child that was just learning how to walk. The child snuggled up to Jesus, and tugged at his beard. Jesus laughed.

"Look at this child. This child doesn't know who I am. But the child can feel my love. And so the child trusts me. That's what God's Shalom is like."

Then Jesus gave the child a little hug and a kiss.

But some of the grownups still didn't understand.

Zacchaeus Climbs a Tree

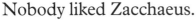

Luke 19:1-9

Nobody liked Zacchaeus.

His job was to get taxes from people.
The Roman soldiers who were in the country said, "Everybody
has to pay us money." Zacchaeus worked for the Romans. His
job was to get tax money from the people and give it to the
Romans.

Zacchaeus sometimes took extra money and kept it for
himself. So Zacchaeus was very rich. But nobody liked
Zacchaeus.

One day Jesus came to the town where Zacchaeus lived.
Excited people lined up on the side of the road. They wanted
to see Jesus.

Zacchaeus had heard that Jesus was a famous teacher.
He wanted to see Jesus too.

But Zacchaeus had a problem. Zacchaeus was short. He
couldn't see anything. When he stood by the side of the road,
all he could see was people's backs.

Zacchaeus didn't know what to do. Then he saw a big tree
near the road. "Aha!" said Zacchaeus. "I'll climb that tree.
Then I can see Jesus!"

Jesus walked into the town. He was smiling and talking to
many people in the crowd. Then Jesus looked up and saw
Zacchaeus in the tree. "Zacchaeus!" said Jesus. "Come down.
Why don't you and I have lunch together at your house?"

"Me?" said Zacchaeus. He was so surprised, he almost fell
out of the tree. The people in the crowd were surprised too.
"Zacchaeus takes our money and gives it to the Romans," they
said. "Why would Jesus want to be friends with him?"

Zacchaeus and Jesus had lunch together. They talked about
living in God's way. "Up until now, I only cared about myself,"

said Zacchaeus. "No wonder nobody liked me. I didn't like myself."

"I'm glad you feel differently," said Jesus. "Are you going to live differently?"

Zacchaeus thought for a long time. Then he looked at Jesus and said, "Yes. I have too much money and too many things. I'm going to give half of it to poor people."

"That's good," said Jesus. "Is there anything else?"

Again, Zacchaeus thought for a long time. "I often took more money from people than I should have. I cheated them. So I'm going to give back four times what I took from them."

Jesus took Zacchaeus' hand. "Something very important has happened, Zacchaeus. You've just learned about God's Shalom."

Jesus Goes to Jerusalem

Matthew 21:1-11, 14-16
Mark 11:1-11
Luke 19:28-40
John 12:12-19

"Have you heard about Jesus?" people were saying. "Have you heard about the things he says and does? Everybody knows Jesus!"

Jesus was becoming very famous. Some people began to wonder, "Is Jesus the Messiah? Is this the one God promised?"

Many people thought the Messiah would be like an army general. The Messiah would gather soldiers and fight the Romans. The Messiah would kill the people they didn't like.

Some of Jesus' disciples, like Peter, were sure Jesus was the Messiah. But even Peter sometimes thought the Messiah would be a general.

Because Jesus was famous, crowds of people came to see him wherever he went. So Jesus decided to show the people something important.

"I am going to go into Jerusalem," Jesus said to his disciples. "I want you to get me a donkey, so I can ride it into the city."

"A donkey? Why not a big, strong horse?"

"No, a donkey. A small, young donkey. I don't want to go into Jerusalem like a general on a horse. I don't want to fight. If I ride on a donkey, people will know that I am coming to bring peace."

The crowds gathered on both sides of the road when they heard Jesus was coming. They cheered and shouted as Jesus rode into Jerusalem. Some of them threw down their clothes so the donkey could walk on something soft. Others cut down some branches from trees for the donkey to walk on.

"Hosanna! Hosanna!" shouted the crowds. Hosanna means "Save us now."

Jesus didn't like that. "They still think I'm going to be a general," he thought. "They think I've come to fight the Romans."

Most of the rulers didn't understand Jesus either. They thought a Messiah had to be a general who would fight people. They didn't understand what Jesus was trying to show them when he rode into the city on a donkey.

When the rulers heard the people shout "Hosanna! Save us now!" they began to feel afraid.

"If Jesus is going to be the Messiah, then he will be the ruler instead of us. We'd better find a way to kill him. Soon!"

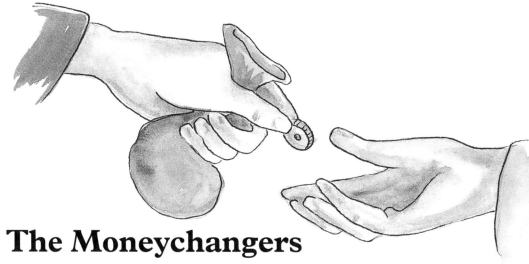

The Moneychangers

Matthew 21:12-13
Mark 11:15-18
Luke 19:45-48

Jesus wanted to pray in the Temple in Jerusalem. The Temple was the biggest church in the whole country.

Jesus walked around the Temple. It was very beautiful. But Jesus saw something there that made him feel angry.

People came to the Temple to worship God. As part of their worship, they gave some money. They needed a special kind of money to take inside the Temple. The people got this special money from moneychangers. The moneychangers took ordinary money, and gave people the Temple money.

Some of the moneychangers cheated people. Especially the poor people. And that made Jesus very angry.

Jesus walked right up to the moneychangers. He grabbed their tables and turned them over. The money rolled all over the floor.

"Don't you know?" Jesus yelled at them. "This is God's house. It should be a place where everyone comes to pray. But you are making it a den of robbers!"

The moneychangers scrambled all over trying to pick up their money. Then they went to the rulers. "Did you see what Jesus did?" they cried.

"That Jesus!" said the rulers. "We've got to get rid of him. Somehow."

Jesus the Servant

Matthew 26:17-19
Mark 14:12-16
Luke 22:7-13, 24-29

Jesus had come to Jerusalem for a very special reason. He wanted to celebrate the Passover there.

Jewish people celebrate the Passover to remember the time God helped them escape from Egypt.

Jesus said to his disciples, "Go find a place where we can eat together. Get the food ready, so we can have our Passover."

Near the end of the day, Jesus and the disciples got together in a nice room they had found. All the food was ready.

Jesus wanted the disciples to know this would be a very special Passover. "Some important things are going to happen soon," he said. "This may be the last time I eat with you."

The disciples weren't really listening. They were arguing.

"I'm better than you are!" one of them said.

"You are not!"

"I am so!"

"My friends, please!" said Jesus. "That's the way people argue when they don't know about living in God's way. But that's not the way you should be.

"In God's Shalom, things are different. The one who is weakest is more important than the one who is strongest. The one who is poorest is loved more than the one who is rich.

"I am your servant. I have come to help you and to help others. That's what a servant does. I'm not here to be your boss. I don't want to be your ruler. I want to be your friend."

The disciples tried hard to understand. But it didn't make sense. Jesus is the Messiah, God's chosen one. How can the boss be a servant?

Washing Feet

John 13:1-20

"What are you doing?" Peter asked. Jesus had poured some water into a basin. Then Jesus tied a towel around his waist.

"I'm going to wash your feet," said Jesus.

"What?" said Peter. "You shouldn't do that. Let me call a servant. It's a servant's job to wash feet."

Jesus and the disciples lived in a hot, dry country. The roads were very dusty. A few rich people rode along the road on horses. A few people got to ride on donkeys. But most people walked when they needed to go somewhere. Their feet got hot and tired and dirty.

When people came to visit, they liked to have their feet washed. It made them feel clean and rested. Rich people had servants who washed feet. Important people didn't wash feet.

That's why Peter thought it was awful when Jesus said, "I'm going to wash your feet."

"No," said Peter. "You will never wash my feet."

"Peter," said Jesus, "God wants me to be your servant. When I am your servant, and you are my servant, then we can really be friends."

"I want to be friends more than anything," said Peter. "You can wash me all over if it will help us be friends."

"Just your feet," smiled Jesus. So Jesus washed Peter's feet. Then he washed the other disciples' feet too.

When he finished, Jesus explained.

"Sometimes you call me Teacher and sometimes you call me Lord. That's fine. That's what I am. But when I washed your feet, I showed you that I am also your servant.

"You should wash each other's feet too. You should be servants to each other. I have showed you how to live in God's way. Be each other's servants."

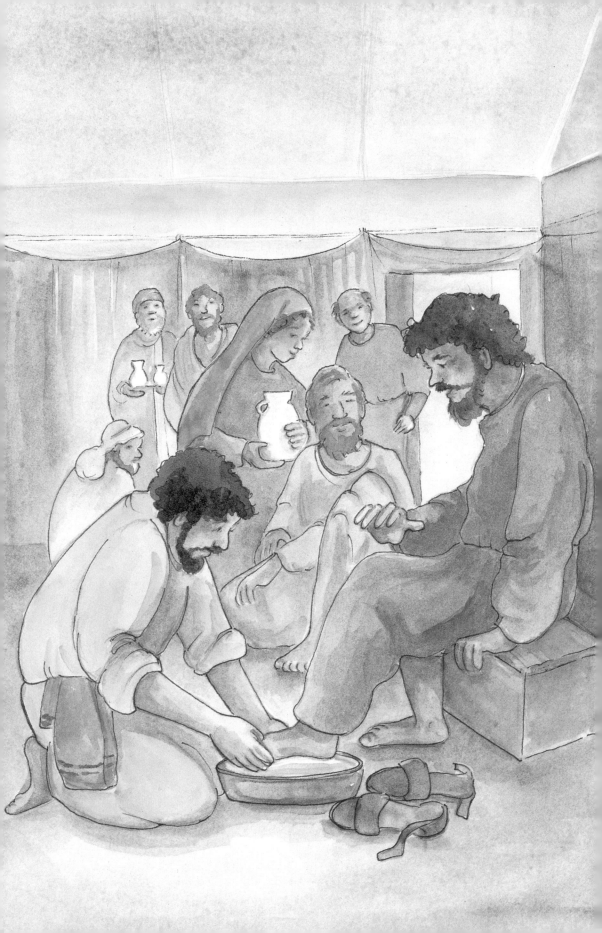

A Warning

Matthew 26:20-25, 31-35
Mark 14:17-21, 27-31
Luke 22:21-23, 31-34
John 13:21-38

All the disciples stopped talking. They couldn't believe what Jesus had just said.

"One of you has stopped being my friend," Jesus told them. "One of you will try to hurt me. One of you will betray me."

Jesus and the disciples were having the special Passover meal together. They were having a good time. And now Jesus said this terrible thing was happening to them.

"But who would do this?" asked one of the disciples.

"The one that I give this piece of bread to," said Jesus. And Jesus gave the bread to Judas.

Judas stood straight up. He looked right at Jesus. "How did you know?" he asked.

"Judas, do what you have to do. But do it quickly."

Judas rushed out of the room.

For a long time, nobody said a word. Then Jesus spoke.

"My children," he said very softly. "I have to go away from you.

"I want you to remember one thing that is more important than anything else. Love one another. Love one another the way I love you. That's the only way people will know that you are my disciples – my friends. Love one another."

"But where are you going?" Peter asked.

"Where I'm going, you cannot come. At least, not now. Later you can come and be with me again.

"Something is going to happen tonight," said Jesus. "Some of you will say you are not my friends."

"Oh no!" said Peter. "I would never do that."

"Peter," said Jesus. "Before the rooster crows in the morning, you will say, 'I don't know him,' three times."

"Never," said Peter. "I would rather die first."

The Last Supper

Matthew 26:26-29
Mark 14:22-25
Luke 22:17-20
1 Corinthians 11:23-26

Peter's head was spinning.
So much had happened that
night. The disciples and
Jesus had come together to
have their Passover supper.

At first there was lots of
happy talk. Peter had even tried to tell a joke, but of course he
didn't get it right. Peter was never good at telling jokes.

Peter noticed that Jesus seemed very quiet. "It looks as if
Jesus is hurting deep down inside," Peter thought.

The meal was almost over when they found out that Judas
would try to hurt Jesus. They wondered what Judas would do.
They were afraid. Very afraid. They knew the rulers had been
trying to get rid of Jesus. Would Judas help them?

Then Jesus spoke. He spoke ever so quietly, but the disciples
heard every single word.

"My dear friends," he said. "Let's say 'thank you' to God for
this meal. Let's pray together.

"O God, thank you for this food. Amen."

Then Jesus took a loaf of bread. He broke it into pieces and
gave a piece to each of the disciples.

"Think of this bread as my body," Jesus said. "It will be broken for you."

Then Jesus picked up the wine. "Think of this wine as my blood. My blood will be poured out for you." Then Jesus gave each of the disciples some of the wine to drink.

"Do you remember the promise God made to Abraham and Sarah and to all the Hebrew people? It was God's covenant. God promised to love us always. To be with us forever. And God gave us a rainbow so we would remember that covenant.

"I am giving you God's promise again. A new covenant from God. From now on, whenever you eat and drink, remember God's covenant. Live in God's way. Live the way I showed you."

Jesus Prays in the Garden

Matthew 26:30, 36-46
Mark 14:26, 32-42
Luke 22:39-46
John 18:1

Jesus and the disciples finished their Passover meal. They sang a
song, and then went to a place called the Mount of Olives. The
night was very dark. All of them were worried and afraid, so they
sang quietly as they walked.

They came to a garden called Gethsemane. "Please sit here
under the trees," Jesus said to the disciples. "I want to go over there
and pray. Peter, James, John... would you three come with me?

This is a hard time for me. I need some of my friends
near me."

The four of them walked over to a lonely place. The night
was dark but Peter could see that Jesus was crying. "I am
worried and afraid," Jesus said to Peter. "Please stay with me
while I pray to God."

Peter, James and John had seen Jesus pray many times, but
they had never seen him pray so hard.

"Oh God!" Jesus was face down on the ground. He was
almost shouting. "My Father, oh my Father, does this have to
happen? Isn't there any way I can get out of this?"

Jesus was quiet for a long while. Then, almost in a whisper
he said, "Not what I want, God, but what you want."

When Jesus finished praying, he looked over at Peter, James
and John. They were asleep. Jesus woke them. "Couldn't you
just stay awake with me for a little while?" he said sadly. "Never
mind. I understand. In your mind you want to stay awake, but
your body is too tired."

Jesus began to pray again. "My Father. If these things have
to happen to me...well..." He stood very quietly for a long time,
listening for what God would say to him. Then Jesus whispered,
"I will do what you want me to do."

Jesus looked at his disciples. They were asleep again. This
time Jesus didn't even try to wake them up. He just began to
pray some more.

Jesus prayed to God for a long time. He didn't say many
words. Mostly he seemed to be listening.

Then he went back and woke up his disciples.
"Wake up! The time has come. Here come the people who
want to kill me."

Jesus Is Arrested

Matthew 26:47-56
Mark 14:43-50
Luke 22:47-53
John 18:2-12

Jesus heard them coming.
The disciples heard them too.

Soldiers were marching into
the garden. Leading them
was Judas.

The rulers had paid Judas
some money. "Help us to catch Jesus," they said. "We must do
it when there aren't many people around. His friends might try
to stop us."

"I know a quiet garden where Jesus and his friends go at
night," said Judas. "I will lead the soldiers there. It will be dark
and hard to see. I will go and kiss Jesus so the soldiers know
who to catch."

"Who are you looking for?" Jesus called to the soldiers. "If
you are looking for me, then let my friends go."

Judas came right up to Jesus. "Hello, teacher," he said. And
he gave Jesus a kiss.

"Judas," said Jesus. "You help the soldiers catch me by
giving me a kiss?"

Then the soldiers grabbed Jesus. Peter had a sword and he
wanted to fight the soldiers. But Jesus said, "No, Peter. Put
your sword away. People who kill will be killed themselves. This
terrible thing has to happen."

Then Jesus said to the soldiers, "I was in the temple every
day. Why didn't you come and get me there? I don't have any
army. I don't even have a sword. Why do you come with all
those swords and clubs?"

The soldiers didn't say anything. Judas didn't say anything.
They just tied Jesus' hands and took him away.

And all of the disciples ran away. Even Peter.

"I Don't Know Him!"

Matthew 26:58, 69-75
Mark 14:54, 66-72
Luke 22:54-62
John 18:15-18, 25-27

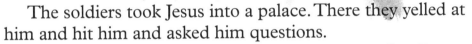

Peter ran away when they arrested Jesus. But then, Peter turned around and started following. Peter felt afraid and brave at the same time. "I will find a way to save Jesus from the soldiers," he thought. But he was afraid to try anything.

The soldiers took Jesus into a palace. There they yelled at him and hit him and asked him questions.

Outside of the palace some people had a campfire. It was very late at night and Peter felt very cold. He went to the fire to get warm.

A girl looked at Peter. "Aren't you one of Jesus' friends?" she asked.

"I don't know what you're talking about," said Peter. And he turned his back to the girl.

Then another one of the people looked at Peter. "Hey! You were with Jesus!"

"I don't know him!" shouted Peter.

It was very cold. Peter could see a little bit of light in the sky. It would soon be morning. The people standing around the fire could see each other better.

Some of them were looking at Peter. "Sure is cold out here," Peter said. He was trying to be friendly.

"You talk just like Jesus talks," said one of the men. "You must be one of his friends."

"I am not," Peter screamed. "I don't know him! I've never heard of him! I am not his friend!"

Just then, Peter heard the rooster crow. Peter remembered.

Peter remembered that Jesus had said, "Before the rooster crows in the morning, you will say, 'I don't know him!' three times." Jesus knew that Peter would be afraid.

Peter walked away from the warm campfire. He felt all cold inside. Peter began to cry.

"Jesus Must Be Killed"

Matthew 27:2, 11-26
Mark 15:1-15
Luke 23:1-5, 13-25
John 18:28 – 19:16

The Pharisees and the other rulers had arrested Jesus. They wanted to kill him.

They took Jesus to the man who was in charge of the whole country. His name was Pilate. He was from another country called Rome. Only Pilate could have people killed.

"Why do you want me to kill Jesus?" Pilate asked.

"Because Jesus says he is the Messiah," said the rulers. "A Messiah is like a king. If Jesus is a king, then we should obey him instead of you."

Pilate decided to talk to Jesus himself. "Are you a king?" he asked.

"Why did you ask that?" said Jesus. "Did those other rulers tell you I was a king?"

"Well, are you?" Pilate asked.

"In a way, I am a king," said Jesus. "But I am not the kind of king who wants to be powerful. I am not the kind of king who has an army."

"Then how are you a king?" asked Pilate.

"I have come to show people how to live in God's way. That's why I was born. I want people to know what is true and what is good. Those who want to know what is true listen to me. They will not always obey you or the other rulers."

Pilate thought for a long time about what Jesus had said. Then Pilate went back to the rulers. "I don't think he has done anything so bad that we need to kill him."

"No, no," cried the rulers. "Jesus must be killed."

The rulers had gone all around Jerusalem and brought crowds to Pilate's palace. Some of the people had watched Jesus ride into Jerusalem on a donkey. They had shouted "Hosanna!"

Now the rulers wanted the crowd to help get Jesus killed. So when Pilate came to the door of his palace, they all yelled, "Kill him! Kill him! Kill him!"

"But why?" said Pilate.

The crowd just kept yelling. "Kill him! Kill him! Kill him!"

Pilate thought, "Maybe if I punish Jesus, that will make the crowd and the rulers happy."

So Pilate told the soldiers to hit Jesus. The soldiers hit Jesus with sticks until he was bleeding. They teased him and dressed him up like a king. They put a crown on Jesus' head. It was a crown made of sharp thorns that hurt his head.

Then the soldiers laughed at Jesus. "Look at our wonderful king," they yelled.

Pilate told the crowd and the rulers what he had done. But they still kept yelling, "Kill him! Kill him! Kill him!"

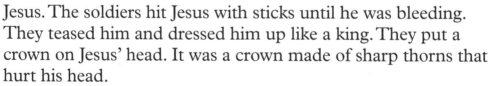

So Pilate went to talk to Jesus again. "Who are you, really? Don't you know that I have the power to kill you?"

"You have no power except the power that God has given you," said Jesus.

Pilate shook his head. He was afraid of all those people. So he said to the rulers, "Here is your king. Do what you want with him. Kill Jesus if you want."

Then Pilate took a basin of water. He washed his hands so that everyone could see what he was doing. "Look," Pilate yelled. "My hands are clean. It's not my fault that Jesus is going to die."

Jesus Is Killed

Matthew 27:31-56
Mark 15:20-37
Luke 23:26-46
John 19:16-30

The soldiers teased
Jesus. They beat Jesus.
Then the rulers of
Jerusalem said to the soldiers, "Take him out and kill him."

The soldiers had a cross. The cross was made of two very heavy pieces of wood. It was a very cruel way to kill people. To make it even worse the soldiers said to Jesus, "You carry the cross."

After the terrible beating, Jesus could hardly walk. He couldn't carry the heavy cross. The solders grabbed a man called Simon of Cyrene and made him help. Simon had to carry the cross all the way to the garbage dump, a place called Golgotha. The soldiers often took people to Golgotha to kill them.

The soldiers laid the cross on the ground. They took a big hammer and nailed Jesus to the cross. Then the soldiers raised it up. Jesus hung there by the nails through his hands and his feet. It hurt terribly.

Jesus looked at the soldiers who were doing this awful thing. Jesus thought about Pilate and the other rulers who made it happen. "Father," Jesus prayed to God, "forgive them. They don't understand what a terrible thing they are doing."

The soldiers and the people walking by began teasing Jesus again.

"Hey, you!" they yelled. "If you're the Messiah, save yourself."

"Yeah," called another. "If you really are God's chosen one, come down off that cross."

Jesus didn't say anything. But he looked down from the cross and saw his mother, Mary. She was crying. One of the disciples was standing nearby. "Please take care of my mother," Jesus said to the disciple.

It seemed like such a long time that Jesus hung there on the cross. The pain got worse and worse.

"My God," Jesus screamed. "My God, why have you left me all alone?"

Then, after a while, when only those standing very close could hear him, Jesus said, "Father, I am ready to die. I put my spirit into your hands."

And Jesus died.

Mary of Magdala Sees Jesus

John 20:1-18

Mary of Magdala had been one of Jesus' friends.

Mary didn't run away when the rulers killed Jesus. She and some of the other women disciples stayed near Jesus all the time that he hung on the cross.

Mary wanted so much to help Jesus. But the soldiers wouldn't let her.

Now Jesus was dead. Mary felt as if she had died too.

Early on Sunday morning, on the third day after Jesus had been killed, Mary went to the place where they had put Jesus' dead body. But when she got there, she saw that Jesus' body was gone.

Mary was very upset. She ran to call some of Jesus' other disciples. They came running as fast as they could. They too saw that Jesus' dead body wasn't there anymore.

Jesus' other friends didn't know what to do, so they went home. Mary stayed behind. She wanted to be by herself for a while. She wanted to have a good cry. Mary was very sad about all the things that had happened to Jesus.

While she was crying, she looked into the place where they had put Jesus' body. She saw two angels. The angels asked her, "Why are you crying?"

"They have taken Jesus away," said Mary. "And I don't know where they have put him."

Then Mary turned around, and she saw somebody standing there. She was still crying, and the tears in her eyes made it hard for her to see who it was.

"Who are you looking for?" this person asked. "And why are you crying?"

Mary cried even harder. "If you have taken Jesus away, please tell me where you have put him, and I will go and get him."

"Mary," he said.

As soon as she heard her name, she knew who it was.

"Teacher!" she shouted. She was so happy. Jesus had been dead but now he was alive again.

"Go and tell the other disciples," said Jesus. "Tell them that I am going to live with God."

So Mary of Magdala went running just as fast as she could – running and jumping and shouting because she was so happy.

Jesus was alive again!

On the Road to Emmaus

Luke 24:13-35

"I can't figure it out," said Cleopas. "Peter says Jesus' body is gone. And Mary says she saw Jesus. She says Jesus isn't dead any more."

"I don't believe that," said the other disciple. "When someone is killed they are dead. They can't come alive again!"

It was the Sunday after Jesus was killed. The two disciples were going along the road to a town called Emmaus. As they walked a stranger came and walked with them. They didn't know who he was.

"What are you talking about?" asked the stranger. "And why are you so sad?"

"Where have you been?" asked Cleopas. "Are you the only one who doesn't know about all the things that happened?"

"What things?" asked the stranger.

"The rulers," said Cleopas. "And the soldiers. They hated Jesus. They killed Jesus."

"Why did they hate Jesus?" the stranger wanted to know.

"Who knows? Maybe they thought Jesus was going to start an army and fight them. Jesus told us he would be killed. Then Jesus said he would come alive again in three days. That's pretty hard to believe. Anyway, here it is, the third day since he was killed. Mary of Magdala says he's alive, but I don't believe her. As far as we know, Jesus is dead."

Then the stranger began to talk to them. The stranger told the story of Moses and all the prophets. "Do you find it hard to believe that Jesus was killed?" asked the stranger. "Do you find it hard to believe that he came alive again?"

"Yeah. We sure do," said Cleopas.

The three of them reached the town of Emmaus. "Why don't you come in and stay with us?" they said to the stranger. "It's almost dark outside. Besides, you must be hungry."

Soon they were ready to have a meal together.

Then the stranger took a piece of bread, and broke it. He gave Cleopas and the other disciple pieces of the bread.

Suddenly Cleopas remembered. He remembered the last supper Jesus had with his friends. He remembered how Jesus had broken the bread.

"It's you!" shouted Cleopas. "It's you, Jesus. You're alive!"

And the stranger was gone.

"We should have known," said Cleopas. "When we were walking along. The way he talked to us. I felt warm and good inside as I listened to him. We should have known it was Jesus. We should have believed what Mary told us!"

The Disciples Believe

Mark 16:14
Luke 24:33-48
John 20:19-23

"I hope the other disciples believe us," said Cleopas as they hurried back along the road to Jerusalem. It was dark. They didn't feel safe. But the disciples wanted to go to Jerusalem quickly. They wanted to tell the others that Jesus was alive.

When they got there, the other disciples didn't believe them. Not at first. Cleopas kept saying, "But we saw him ourselves. And Mary of Magdala saw Jesus too! Can't you believe us?"

Peter and the others wanted to believe Mary. They wanted to believe Cleopas. They wanted Jesus to be alive. But how could such a thing happen?

Then, all of a sudden, he was there. Jesus was there in the room with them. "Peace!" said Jesus. "Peace be with you."

"It must be a ghost!" said Peter.

"No, I am not a ghost," said Jesus. "Touch me. Feel my hands and my feet. A ghost doesn't have bones and skin. And you can see the places where I'm bleeding. There are bleeding holes in my hands and in my feet where the soldiers nailed me to the cross."

"Wow!" said Peter. "You *are* alive. You're alive, just as you said you would be."

"I'm alive," said Jesus. "And I'd like something to eat."

Then Jesus sat down with the disciples. They had lunch and a long, long talk. Jesus explained many things to them. He told the disciples how the story of Abraham and Sarah, the story of Moses and Miriam, of Isaiah and Jeremiah, were all part of God's story. "It's the story of how God loves you and everybody," said Jesus.

"And when you do wrong," said Jesus, "and you say 'I'm sorry' to God, God will give you another chance. You can try again to live in God's way."

Thomas Asks Questions

Based on John 14:1-7, 20:24-29

"Don't ask so many questions, Thomas."
   That's what Thomas' teachers said in school.
   That's what Thomas' parents said at home.
   That's what Thomas' friends said.

   But Thomas couldn't help it. When the Rabbi, the teacher, told them things in school Thomas often asked, "How do you know?"
   Sometimes that made the Rabbi angry. "I know just because I know, Thomas. It is true because I say so."
   Thomas had to be quiet, but he didn't like the teacher's answer. Thomas was sad when his questions made people angry. But he couldn't stop asking.

When Thomas grew older, he became one of Jesus' special friends. He became a disciple. Thomas liked Jesus, because Jesus never told him to stop asking questions.

One day Jesus was trying to explain what was going to happen. "I am going away," said Jesus. "I am going to get a place ready for you. God's house has room for you and for everyone else. You know the way to God's house."

"No we don't," said Thomas. "What is the way?"

"That's a good question, Thomas," smiled Jesus. "I am the way. If you really love me, and love each other, then you know the way."

"I still don't understand all of it," said Thomas.

"That's okay," said Jesus. "Just keep asking questions."

Not long after that, Jesus died. He was killed by people who didn't like the way he said that God loved everyone. Thomas was very sad when Jesus was killed, so when some of the other disciples said Jesus was alive again, Thomas really wanted to believe them.

But he couldn't. His mind kept asking questions. "How can somebody be dead and then be alive again?" When some of the disciples told Thomas they had seen Jesus, Thomas asked, "How can you be sure it was Jesus? How do you know it wasn't somebody else?"

"But we saw him with our own eyes," said the disciples.

"Maybe," said Thomas. "But I have to see for myself. I have to see the places in Jesus' hands where they put the nails. Otherwise I won't believe it."

A few days later, Thomas and his friends were together. All the doors were closed, but suddenly, there was Jesus in the room with them. He smiled at Thomas. "Come here, my friend. Touch the places where they put the nails. It really *is* me."

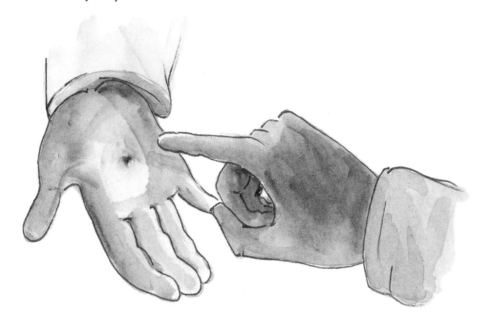

Thomas began to cry, he was so happy to see Jesus. "Oh, yes, it is you Jesus. I am so glad. Now I know that you are alive again. I won't ask any more questions."

"Oh, don't stop asking questions, Thomas," said Jesus. "I am glad you are able to see me so you can be sure. Then you can believe. But there will be lots of people who won't be able to see me. They will ask questions too. It will be hard for them to believe, just as it was hard for you to believe. I will need you to help tell them my story."

"You mean, you're not angry because I didn't believe right away that you were alive again?" Thomas asked.

"No, not angry at all," said Jesus. "I like it when people ask hard questions. But you won't understand everything, Thomas. You will never find answers to *all* your questions. Just remember that I love you and that God loves you. Nobody can prove that part, but it is the part that is the most true."

Peter Learns

John 21:1-17

Peter was tired. He had been fishing all night long.

"We haven't caught a thing," said Peter. "We might as well row back to the shore."

It was several weeks after Jesus had been killed. The disciples got together often to talk about Jesus and to remember the things he had said and done.

"I wonder what Jesus wants us to do now?" Peter often asked the other disciples. "He lived with us here. He taught us many things about God and about each other. Then Jesus was killed, but we know he's alive again. So what? What do we do now?"

On this night, the disciples had gone fishing together. But there didn't seem to be any fish.

Peter heard a voice calling from the shore. It was still quite dark. Peter couldn't see who it was.

"My friends," called the voice. "Have you caught any fish?"

"None at all!" Peter called back.

"Put your net on the other side of the boat," the voice called. "You'll find some fish there."

That's what they did. In no time at all, the net was so full of fish, they thought it would break.

"I know who that is," said one of the disciples. "That's Jesus. Who else knows where the fish are?"

Peter got very excited. He jumped into the water and swam

to shore. The other disciples rowed the boat up to the beach. It was hard, because they had so very many fish. "There were 153 fish in that net," said Thomas.

"Bring some of the fish here," said Jesus. "We'll cook them for breakfast." Jesus had built a nice little fire on the shore.

"Mmmm, these really taste good," said Peter. Jesus laughed. He looked at Peter with his mouth so full of fish. Then, suddenly, Jesus looked a little sad.

"Peter," said Jesus. "Do you love me?"

"Sure," said Peter. "You know that."

"Then feed my lambs," said Jesus.

Jesus didn't say anything for a while. Peter kept on eating fish, but he wondered what Jesus meant.

"Peter," said Jesus. "Do you really love me?"

"Of course, Jesus," said Peter. "You know I love you."

"Take care of my sheep," said Jesus.

Jesus was quiet again. Peter had stopped eating. He was thinking hard about what Jesus had said.

After a while, Jesus spoke again. He spoke so quietly, Peter could hardly hear.

"Peter, do you love me?"

Peter began to feel a little hurt. Why did Jesus keep asking him the same question? "You know everything, Jesus," he said. "You know that I love you."

"Feed my sheep."

That was the last time that Peter and the other disciples saw Jesus. But they knew he was alive.

Jesus was alive in their hearts. The disciples felt Jesus was somehow with them whenever they talked about him. When they prayed, they knew Jesus was listening to their prayers.

And many, many times, Peter thought about that last time with Jesus. And he could hear Jesus saying to him, "Feed my sheep." And Peter knew what he had to do.

Peter knew Jesus wanted him to feed God's sheep, to help people live in God's way.

Birthday of the Church

Acts 2

It was seven weeks since Jesus died. But the disciples knew Jesus was still alive.

One day the disciples were all together, with many other people. It was the day of Pentecost, an important time for Jewish people.

Then something very strange happened. Some said there was the sound of a strong wind. Others said there were little bits of fire dancing around among the disciples.

The strangest part was that the disciples began to talk in new ways. Nobody was sure what kind of languages they spoke. Even the disciples weren't sure about the new words they heard themselves saying.

But others understood. "Hey!" someone said. "I come from a place where we speak a different language. How come I can understand what he's saying?"

People were there from many far away places. They understood many different languages. They could each understand what the disciples were saying.

"What is going on here?" people asked.

"You drank too much wine!" somebody said to Peter.

"No," said Peter. Then he stood up and talked to all the people who had come together for Pentecost.

"My friends," said Peter, "we're not drunk. Something very important has happened here." Then Peter told them the whole story beginning many, many years ago with Abraham and Sarah, right up till the time of Jesus. Then Peter told them how Jesus was God's Messiah.

Peter explained that from now on, God's spirit would be with everyone who believed in Jesus. We would not be able to see Jesus alive again the way the disciples had seen him. But Jesus would be alive in our hearts. Peter called it "the holy spirit."

"What should we do?" someone asked.

"Be sorry for the wrong things you have done," said Peter. "Believe that God really loves you."

Many people said "Yes, we want to do that." So they were baptized in water. Being baptized was a way of saying "I want to live in God's way."

The disciples were happy. Now they knew what Jesus wanted them to do. Jesus wanted the disciples to help everyone know about God's love.

So the disciples went to many places. They told people about Jesus and about God's promise.

Many people came to the disciples and said, "Yes, I believe that Jesus is God's Messiah. I want to live in God's way."

Soon there were people in many places who knew about Jesus. These people got together to help each other, to eat together, to remember the things that Jesus said, and to talk about living in God's way. When people came together like this, they called it a church.

Sharing

Acts 4:32 – 5:11

The disciples went to different places and told many people about Jesus. Soon there were lots of people who were trying to live in God's way.

They would get together often to talk about Jesus, to have a meal together, and to help each other.

They sometimes talked about Jesus as "The Christ." Christ is another word for Messiah. Because they talked about Christ they were sometimes called Christians. Or they were called "People of the Way," because they tried to live in God's way.

When the Christians got together, they would remember the things Jesus said. Then they would ask, "What would Jesus want us to do?"

One day someone said, "Some of us are rich and some of us are poor. Would Jesus like that?"

"I don't think so," said another. "Why don't we try to share everything?"

So that's what the first Christians did. The ones who were rich brought their money. They shared it with people who didn't have as much.

One man, Joseph, sold a field that he owned. He brought the money and shared it with the other people.

Some of the Christians didn't want to share. Sometimes they would just pretend to share, but they would keep most of their money themselves. That made everyone very sad.

Often, when the Christians gathered, they would eat together. Then they would remember the last supper that Jesus ate with the disciples. They would remember that even though they couldn't see Jesus, he was alive in their hearts.

The Story of Stephen

Acts 6:1 – 8:1

Peter and the other disciples wanted everybody to know about
Jesus. They went out on the streets of Jerusalem every day. They
talked to people about Jesus. More and more people were
learning to live in God's way.

The new Christians tried to share everything with each
other. The rich Christians brought food and money. They gave
it to those who didn't have very much. But now there were so
many Christians. Sometimes it was hard to be fair to everyone.

"He got more than I did," one of the Christians said. And
they started arguing.

"Let's choose some people to help us," the disciples said.

"They can make sure everyone gets their share."

One of the people they chose was Stephen. He worked hard
to be sure everybody was treated fairly. Stephen also helped
teach people about Jesus.

The rulers of Jerusalem didn't like the Christians. The rulers didn't believe that Jesus really was the Messiah. Sometimes they put Peter and the other disciples in jail. They beat the disciples with whips. "Stop telling people about Jesus!" they said.

One day, when the rulers heard Stephen talking about Jesus, they got very angry.

"Stephen is saying we should forget about Moses," they said. "Stephen is telling people lies!"

So the rulers went and got Stephen. "Why are you doing this?" they asked him. "Why are you telling people to forget about Moses?"

Stephen tried to explain. He helped the rulers remember the story of how God had been with Moses and Miriam. He talked about the prophets. "You don't listen to them," he said. "You don't live in the way Moses and Miriam and the other prophets asked you to live."

This made the rulers furious. They grabbed Stephen and dragged him out of the city. They threw big stones at him.

"God, forgive them," Stephen prayed to God. "They don't understand."

The rulers threw more and more stones. They killed Stephen.

A man named Saul was standing nearby. He wasn't throwing stones. But Saul helped by taking care of the coats of the people who were throwing stones.

Saul thought, "This is good. Stephen *should* be killed for teaching people about Jesus. We need to get rid of these Christians!"

Saul and the other rulers thought they were doing the right thing. "Jesus is a phony," they said. "He isn't really the Messiah. These Christians have been tricked."

Saul Learns about Jesus

Acts 9:1-19, 22:3-16, 26:4-18

Saul hated Christians. So Saul went to the rulers and said, "Let me go and get those Christians, the ones they call People of the Way. Let me throw them into jail so they don't tell any more lies about Jesus."

The rulers gave Saul a letter. "Saul can put all the Christians in jail," the letter said.

"I'm going to Damascus," said Saul. "There are many Christians in Damascus. I want to throw them into jail. I want them to stop talking about Jesus."

On the way to Damascus a strange thing happened to Saul. Suddenly, he saw a very bright light. It was so bright Saul couldn't see any more. Then Saul heard somebody talking.

"Saul, Saul," said the voice. "Why are you hurting me?"

"Who is this?" Saul asked. He was very afraid.

"I am Jesus, the one you are hurting," said the voice. "Now get up and go into Damascus. I'll tell you what to do later."

When Saul got up from the ground, he was blind. The people who were with Saul helped him walk. They got him into Damascus. But Saul didn't know what to do. He couldn't eat. He couldn't see. He was afraid.

Ananias lived in Damascus. Ananias tried hard to live in God's way.

One day, Ananias knew that God was telling him something. "Go and find a man named Saul. Saul needs your help."

"But Saul is trying to hurt us," said Ananias. "He wants to put Christians in jail."

"Go," God said to Ananias. "Saul has changed. Saul knows about Jesus."

So Ananias went and found Saul. Ananias put his hands on Saul's head and said, "My brother Saul. The spirit of Jesus has come into your heart."

Then Saul opened his eyes. "I can see again!" he shouted. "I can see!"

Ananias took some water and baptized Saul.

"I'm hungry!" said Saul. "And please, Ananias. While I'm eating, tell me more about Jesus."

Now Saul, who had tried to hurt the People of the Way, had become one of them. Soon he began telling others about Jesus. He went to many different places to tell people about Jesus. Saul wrote many letters which are in our Bible.

Saul was Jewish. He told many people who were not Jews about living in God's way. People who are not Jewish say Saul's name another way. They call him Paul.

There is a very short story in the Bible about a person named Dorcas. The Bible only tells us a small part of the story. It says she was a very kind woman who helped many people. So I read what it said about Dorcas in the Bible, and then made the rest of the story up myself.

Why not read about Dorcas in your Bible? You might want to make up your own story about her.

Dorcas and Anna Help Each Other

Acts 9:36-42

"Here," said Dorcas. "Put this on. It will keep you warm at night."

"Oh, thank you," said Anna. "Thank you very much."

Anna was eight years old. She was all by herself. She had no mother and father and no place to live. She had to sleep outside on the street at night.

Dorcas smiled at Anna. "Here's something to eat. You look hungry."

Anna began to eat right away. She was very hungry. Anna hadn't eaten for three whole days. She was also very lonely and afraid.

After Anna had some food, she felt a little better. Dorcas sat down beside her. "Do you have a place to live? Is there anyone to take care of you?"

Anna shook her head.

"Well then," said Dorcas. "Would it be all right if I found you a place to live?"

"Yes, please," said Anna in a tiny voice.

"Would you come and stay with me until we can find you a

home?" Dorcas asked. Anna nodded.

Dorcas took Anna's hand as they walked. It seemed a long way.

Dorcas began to walk more slowly. She wasn't feeling very well. "No matter," said Dorcas to herself. "I'll be fine soon. I've got to find Anna a place to live."

Dorcas could hardly walk by the time she and Anna got to the house. "Anna," said Dorcas, "would you mind if I just lie down for a while. I'm very tired. All I need is a little rest and then I'll be fine."

But Dorcas wasn't fine. She lay down and closed her eyes. She was very, very still. Anna looked closely. She couldn't see Dorcas breathing. Anna was very worried about her new friend.

Anna ran to the door. She saw one of the neighbors outside. "Please," she said. "Please come quickly. Something is wrong."

"Oh, no," said the neighbor when she came inside. "Dorcas is dead!" The neighbor began to cry very loudly.

Soon many other friends heard the crying and came to look. "What will we do?" they cried. "Dorcas was such a friend. Dorcas always showed us how to live in God's way. Look at the coat she made for me when I was cold."

"She was the only friend I had," thought Anna. "Oh God, please don't let her be dead."

Soon many people had come to see Dorcas. They remembered how often she had helped poor people. She had helped them with food and made clothes for them. Dorcas loved and helped anyone who needed her.

Someone had called Peter. "Look at Dorcas," they said to Peter. "We think she's dead."

"Please, would you all leave the room for a while," said Peter. "I'd like to be alone with Dorcas."

Everyone went into the next room. Anna too.

Peter prayed very quietly to God. Peter thanked God for Dorcas. "She showed so many people how to live in God's way," said Peter. "Dorcas helped so many people."

Then Peter looked at Dorcas and said. "We need you, Dorcas. Please get up."

Slowly, Dorcas opened her eyes. She looked at Peter. Peter took her by the hand and helped her out of bed. They walked into the next room where all the people were waiting.

"Look!" the neighbor shouted. "Dorcas is alive!"

"Oh, what's all the fuss," she said, pretending to be angry. "Go home, all of you. Come, Anna. We've got work to do."

When the people were gone, Dorcas looked at Anna. "Please come and sit with me for a little while, Anna. Hold my hand. I feel better. But I need someone to be gentle and kind to me right now. Would you do that Anna?"

Anna snuggled up to Dorcas and closed her eyes. Deep in her heart Anna said, "Thank you, God."

More and more people heard about Jesus. More and more people were learning how to live in God's way. There were groups of Christians in many places. In each place, they would have a church. They didn't have church buildings. When Christian people come together to pray, to sing, and to work together, they are called a church.

So far, most of the people in the Christian church were Jewish. Some of them felt Jesus had only come to help Jewish people.

Peter often wondered about that. Peter felt deep down that maybe God's love should be shared with everyone.

Cornelius Becomes a Christian

Acts 10:1 – 11:18

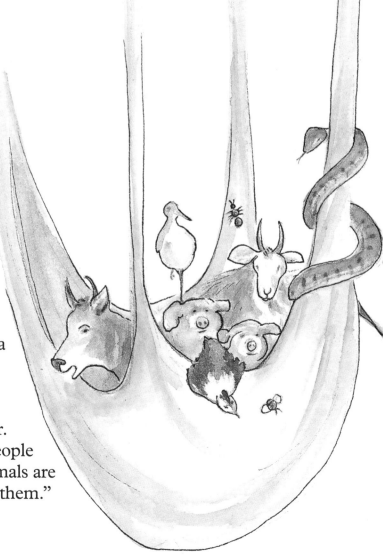

One day while Peter was praying, he saw something strange in his mind.

Peter saw a big cloth coming down from the sky. In the cloth were all kinds of animals. Some of the animals were the kind that Jewish people wouldn't eat.

Then Peter heard a voice. "Take these animals Peter. Cook them and eat them."

"Oh no," said Peter. "I'm Jewish. Jewish people say some of those animals are unclean. We don't eat them."

"Don't say they are unclean," said the voice. "God made them."

Then the big cloth went back up to the sky. But it came back again. And again. It happened three times.

Just then, there was a knock at the door.

"I have a message for Peter," said the man at the door. "Would you come and visit Cornelius? Cornelius would like you to come and see him."

Peter stopped to think. Cornelius was a soldier. Cornelius was not Jewish. "I'm Jewish," thought Peter. "I shouldn't go into the house of someone who isn't Jewish."

Then Peter remembered the big cloth. "God made Cornelius, just as God made me," thought Peter. "I'm not unclean and neither is Cornelius. I think God wants me to go."

Cornelius was very happy when Peter got there. "Thank you for coming," he said. "Please tell me about Jesus."

So Peter told Cornelius and his whole family all about Jesus. Peter talked about the many ways Jesus had showed us how to live in God's way. "God wants us to be kind. We should never hurt each other. The power we have is the power of love."

Peter looked at Cornelius. He looked at the other people in Cornelius' family. Peter could see that the spirit of Jesus had come into their hearts.

"Would you like to be baptized?" Peter asked.

"Yes," they all said. "We want to be baptized. We want to try to live in God's way."

Some of the other Christians were angry when they heard what Peter had done. "Cornelius and his family aren't Jewish," they said. "And Cornelius is a soldier. How can they be People of the Way?"

Peter told them about the big cloth and everything else that had happened. Then everyone understood that God's love is for everybody. They knew that Jesus came to show God's love for the whole world.

"Everyone can learn how to live in God's way," said Peter. "Everyone can be part of the Christian church."

Lydia Starts a New Church

Acts 16:11-40,
Philippians 4:6-9

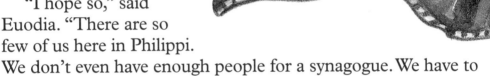

"Look," said Lydia to her friend Euodia. "Those two men walking toward us by the river. Are they Jews?"

"I hope so," said Euodia. "There are so few of us here in Philippi. We don't even have enough people for a synagogue. We have to come down here to the river when we want to pray."

"Hello!" said Lydia to the two men. "Welcome to Philippi. My name is Lydia. This is Euodia."

"My name is Paul," said the man. "And this is my friend Silas. We are looking for the Jewish people who come to the river to pray."

"I wasn't born Jewish," said Lydia. "But I worship the same God. And my friends and I have come here to pray. As you can see, we are five women. A very small group. We would be pleased if you would join us for prayer."

They sang a song first. Then they prayed. They remembered the words of some of the prophets. Soon they were talking about the stories of Abraham and Sarah, about the prophets, and about God's covenant.

It wasn't long before Paul and Silas told Lydia and her friends about Jesus. Paul could see that Lydia was really glad to hear about Jesus.

"That is good news," Lydia said to Paul. "Jesus came to show us what God is like and how to live in God's way. God's love is for everybody. That is really good news."

Paul and Lydia talked some more. Then she said, "Paul, could I be baptized? I really feel the spirit of Jesus is in me, and I do want to live in God's way."

So Paul and Lydia went into the river. Paul dipped Lydia under the water for a moment. He said a prayer to God. "I feel all clean inside," said Lydia.

By this time it was getting late. All of them were feeling hungry.

"Would you come to my place for supper?" Lydia asked.

"Thank you," said Paul. "But we can buy our own food. It would cost too much for you to feed us."

"Don't worry," said Lydia. "I sell purple cloth to people. It's a good business. I have enough money. So come and stay with me."

So Paul and Silas stayed with Lydia during the whole time they were in Philippi. They went around the city and talked about Jesus.

Some of the things they said about Jesus made people angry. Paul and Silas got thrown into jail for a while. Lydia wondered if they would put her in jail too because she helped Paul and Silas. Even though she was a little afraid, Lydia was still glad to have them stay at her house.

Soon Lydia's whole family was baptized into the church, then Euodia and her other friends. Lydia became a leader of a brand new church.

Several years later, Paul wrote a letter to the church that Lydia started. The letter to the Philippians is in our Bible.

"Jesus is always near us," wrote Paul in his letter, "so we don't need to ever be afraid.

"My friends, whatever is true, whatever is right, whatever is lovely, whatever is good...think about these things. When you do, God's peace will be with you."

Here is part of a letter Paul wrote. He wrote it to people in Corinth who sometimes argued with each other. Paul wanted them to work together.

Paul Writes a Letter

1 Corinthians 1:10, 12:4-31

Dear friends in Corinth,
We all like to have things our own way. Each of us would like to be boss over everybody else. But we are a Christian church. We must work together if we want to live in God's way.

Think of your church as if it is a person's body. The whole church body should live in God's way. Not just some parts of it.

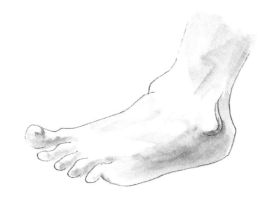

Would your foot say, "Because I am not a hand, I don't belong to the body"?

That's silly.

Would your ear say, "Because I am not an eye, I don't belong to the body"?

That's silly.

If your whole body were an eye, how would you hear things?

If your whole body were an ear, how would you smell things?

Your eye can't say to your hand, "I don't need you." That's silly.

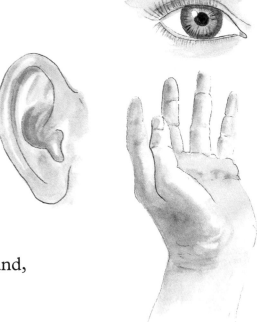

Your head can't say to your feet, "I don't need you." That's silly.

God has put all the parts of our body together so that they help each other. Everything is part of one body.

If part of your body is hurting, then you feel bad all over.

If part of your body is happy, you feel good all over.

The church is like the body of Christ. Each one of us is like the hands, or feet, or eyes, or ears of that body.

Each one of us can do different things. Some people can sing. Others can listen. A few can run fast. Some people can work hard. Others can draw nice pictures. Some people can think about important things.

Each one of us is important. We are Christ's body and we are all needed. Living in God's way means working together as the church.

Your friend,
Paul

Paul wrote many of the letters in our Bible. Other people wrote letters too.
One of the letters in our Bible is called the letter of James. Here is part of it.

Doing God's Work

James 2:4-26

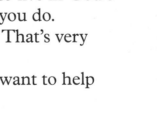

Dear friends all over the world,
Please remember what it
means to live in God's way. It
means you want to *do*
something. It means you want to help if there
is a problem.

Suppose you say, "I love God." But then you
don't *do* anything. You hear about someone who
doesn't have any clothes. Or not enough to eat.

So you say, "Hello! Have a nice day." But you
don't *do* anything. You don't help. You don't try
to find out why they have no clothes. You don't
care why they have no food. What does it mean?

It means you don't really want to live in God's
way. You just want to pretend that you do.

Anybody can say, "I love God." That's very
easy to say.

If you really love God, you will want to help
other people.

Your friend,
James

There was a time when it was very dangerous to be a friend of Jesus. Christians were often hurt, or thrown into jail or killed. The Emperor wanted people to pray to him, as if he were God. Christians didn't want to do that. Jesus had told the Christians about God. They knew the Emperor wasn't God.

Almost a hundred years after Jesus had been born on the earth, a man by the name of John was sent to a lonely island called Patmos. John was taken to this island because he was a Christian.

When John was a prisoner on this island, he wrote a very long letter to his Christian friends. It is the last part of the Bible, and it is called Revelation.

John wanted to help his friends be brave. He knew how hard it was to be a Christian. John wanted his friends to know that even though some people hated them, and though they were often hurt or killed because they were Christian, God had not forgotten them. God was still with them. God loved them. And that a better time was coming when they could worship God without being afraid.

In the book of Revelation, John tells about some strange dreams he had. They seem kind of mixed up and weird to us now, but John's friends knew what they meant. God was helping them through John's strange dreams.

In his dream, John saw a lamb. All the people who read John's letter knew that the lamb was really Jesus, the Messiah.

John's Wonderful Dream

(Revelation Chapters 1, 5, 21, 22 selected verses)

From John
To the seven churches of Asia.

I am John, your brother.
As a follower of Jesus, I have been hurt, just as you have. But I am trying hard not to give up. I keep trusting in God. That is why the rulers sent me away to the island of Patmos.

One day I was having a kind of dream, even though I wasn't really asleep. And I felt that God was inside me, and that God wanted me to write you a letter about it.

I saw a book in the hand of someone sitting on a throne.

But the book was closed up tight, and there was no one to open it.

An angel said in a loud voice, "Who is good enough to open this book?"

Then I saw the Lamb, a Lamb which had been killed. And all the people said:

"You are good enough to open the book,
Because you were killed,
And by dying in this way,
You helped people all over the world
To know about God."

And then I looked again, and I saw angels. Thousands and millions of angels. And they sang this song together:

The Lamb is good enough,
To be given power, and riches,
And wisdom and strength and honor.

Then I saw a new heaven and a new earth. And I saw a Holy City, like the city of Jerusalem. It was as if the whole city was dressed up like a bride at a wedding.

Then I heard a loud voice saying, "God's home is with the people of the world. God will live with them, and they will live with God. God will wipe away all tears from their eyes. There will be no more death. No more crying. No more hurting. Everything will be different.

"Listen to me," said the voice. "I will make all things new. Whoever is thirsty, I will give them a drink from the water of life."

Come. Whoever is thirsty. Here is the water of life. It is a gift to you. It is a gift to whoever wants it.

So it is. Come, Lord Jesus!

May the love of Jesus be with everyone.

Your friend,
John